REVIEWS

of Testimony Is Praise — What's Your Story?

"You'll be entertained, surprised, brought to tears and laughter as you read this honest, heartwarming book about two ordinary people who have lived extraordinary lives. Life's challenges and victories come to us all. John and Donna are no exception. Through their unique individual writing styles and openness to share even their most difficult times, you'll witness the supernatural intervention of God in each chapter. You'll be awed by reading the personal testimonies of what only God can do in the lives of two yielded, obedient King's kids. May their journeys encourage you in your own."

—Janice Buckson, Author of Mining for GOLD in Psalm 91

"A compelling journey of the Spirit of God at work within. John and Donna have found His Spirit time after time. A must-read!"

—Michael Eastman, Director of Kingdom Builders

"Testimony is Praise—What's Your Story? is a wonderful read. I found myself cheering on John and Donna as I read their story about how they are growing in their relationship with Jesus Christ. You will find this book to be transparent, relatable, and inspirational. Definitely a recommended read."

—Pastor Sean Callaghan

"It is amazing to see the fingerprints of where God has been in John and Donna's lives. Life and faith are similar in that they both have their ups and downs, and the Holy Spirit is active and present in both. As their parents and in-laws, we are deeply humbled by their faith story. Yep, these are the kids that God has given to us. As He would say, 'You just got to love 'em.'"

—Pastor David Kipp

"I've known John and Donna for about three years. As they were writing this book, they asked me if I'd like to be one of the proofreaders, to which I replied, "I'd be honored." At the time, I had no idea how wonderfully rewarding it would be to read about their testimonies! They are real, honest, transparent, and clearly filled with the love of God! Reading this book helped my wife and me in our relationship with God, but also with each other! This is a fantastic read; I highly recommend it!"

—Andy Fowler, Retired Sr VP & CIO in healthcare

"John and Donna are two of the most genuine people that I know. Together, they exemplify the complementary relationship the Bible teaches us about. *Testimony Is Praise – What's Your Story* will open your eyes to reflect on your own life and help you understand God is sovereign in all life's circumstances."

—Nate Kneser, Child of God

"*Testimony Is Praise – What's Your Story* offers a fresh insight into life transformation when you put God first in your life and listen to the Holy Spirit. This book is captivating and reading the real-life testimonies of John and Donna's lives will give you the desire to open your ears to hear God's word and open your heart to accept all that He has to offer you!"

—Lori Willy, Small Group Leader

"*Testimony is Praise* is a heart-felt and relational read that demonstrates the power of obedience in following God's purpose He designed for John & Donna's lives. Watching The Holy Spirit transform their hearts through the trials they share in each testimony gives me the desire to surrender all of my life to Him so that I can experience freedom while living a life of pure joy."

—Brad Willy, Small Group Leader

"In the five years we have known the Kipps, we have seen them become increasingly more involved in serving at Bayside Community Church. From lending a hand at a food distribution ministry to leading that ministry. From volunteering with the baptism team to leading the team. From assisting at Bayside's Freedom Ministry to becoming integral leaders there. Their testimony has truly been one of service. We are blessed to consider them friends and you will know them well after reading this book."

—Kevin Kaminski, Small Group Leader

TESTIMONY
IS PRAISE

WHAT'S
YOUR
STORY?

JOHN and DONNA KIPP

All Scripture quotations, unless otherwise indicated, are taken from the Holy Bible, New Living Translation, Copyright © 1996, 2004, 2015 by Tyndale House Foundation. Used by permission of Tyndale House Publishers, Inc., Carol Stream, Illinois 60188. All rights reserved.

Scripture quotations marked (NIV) are taken from the Holy Bible, New International Version®, NIV® Copyright © 1973, 1978, 1984, 2011 by Biblica, Inc.™ Used by permission of Zondervan. All rights reserved worldwide. www.zondervan.com The "NIV" and "New International Version" are trademarks registered in the United States Patent and Trademark Office by Biblica, Inc.™

ISBN 978-0-578-34620-5

Cover and book design by Oleg Atbashian
Cover photo by David Choate - https://david-choate.pixels.com
Edited by Maureen Guffanti

CONTENTS

Come and listen, all you who fear God, and I will tell you what he did for me.

—Psalm 66:16

INTRODUCTION

W hy would anyone want to hear about *our* lives? Most would say there is nothing "special" about us. We're not trained pastors and our friends and family may be disappointed when they hear about our struggles. Clearly, we should never have thought we have anything of value to bring forth, right? No! These are lies the enemy has told us. We were all created by God in His image, and He has a purpose for each of our lives. In this book, we will use Biblical principles woven into our testimony to encourage you to tell *your* story, your experiences of God's faithfulness.

When something happens in life that can only be explained by God being the master orchestrator, some like to call it coincidence, but we like to say those are God stories, or testimonies.

We believe testimony is praise. Our intention is not to focus on ourselves, but to give God glory for what He has done in our lives. We will start each chapter with Scripture, each of our testimonies, a few comments about the topic of the chapter, and then some questions that will help you reflect and will sometimes challenge you to action. You can stop and answer the questions as you complete each chapter—or you could decide to do them after reading the entire book.

John's Testimony

As I walked by the church meeting room one night in February 2016, my friend Brad stopped me. After telling me the speaker for that night's Celebrate Recovery® session had called in sick, Brad said I should give my testimony. I'm a person who likes to plan, even for a simple prayer in front of a group, so I responded with, "I don't have a testimony." How much more wrong could I have been? I didn't speak that night, but the next several months were filled with so many struggles and God stories that a seed was planted for this book.

Perhaps you don't think you have a story either. Maybe you think your life has been unremarkable. Our prayer is this book will be an encouragement to you so you will know your story is important, your story isn't over, and, through your experiences, God has prepared you to help others. Ephesians 2:10 says, "For we are God's masterpiece. He has created us anew in Christ Jesus, so we can do the things He planned for us long ago."

Donna's Testimony

When John said he didn't have a testimony, my first reaction was panic! To me, that meant "his story" would involve me—and I was fairly sure it wasn't going to be pretty.

Fast forward two years and many struggles later, and I was right! Now that John realized he had a testimony, he was convinced that "we" needed to write a book. I naturally said: "Uh, no." Not just no, but NO!!!!!!!!! He expected me to talk about the areas of my life I NEVER talk about. What possible reason could I have to do that? John wrote a brief introduction and chapter outline, but with me not cooperating, he put it aside.

Another year went by. We were at a ministry meeting and a dear friend suddenly said, "I need to tell you guys what the Lord is telling me." First, she asked if we worked together. We said, "No, but we share an office; we both work remotely for two separate companies based in Kentucky." She told us we would be working together on a project and God would take it from there. John immediately said, "It's the book I told you about!" I just said, "Have fun with YOUR book."

The next day, without knowing what we had heard the night before, another friend of ours texted John, "Praying for you, my friend. There is an intersection coming your way. Speak!" John was adamant this time about writing a book together because he was sure he was hearing from God, and I knew he wasn't going to let it go. I had been in this position before, with John and me seriously disagreeing, so I did the same thing I did then: I prayed not to be a stumbling block for John if this was God's will. A few days later, we took a laptop and went to a restaurant to discuss the first chapter. The waitress came by and said, "I don't want to interrupt, but do you mind if I ask what you guys are working on?" John told her the title of the book and the reason for writing it. She said she wanted to read it when we got it finished! She also told us she had just moved here and didn't have a church home. We gave her our number and invited her to come to church with us.

I was still struggling with the book's topics and what to say, but I could no longer argue since John had received confirmation from three separate people in a week's time. I asked Holy Spirit why He spoke through someone else instead of telling *me*. He simply said, "If I asked *you* to write a book, would you?"

I knew I wouldn't have. The God stories you will read are just a glimpse of what God has been doing in our lives—including what happened during the book writing process!

So . . . let's start at the beginning!

For every child of God defeats this evil world, and we achieve this victory through our faith.

—1 John 5:4

Chapter 1

CHILDHOOD BAGGAGE

Donna's Testimony

Heart pounding, I came awake . . . what had I heard? A loud thud? I sat up. At my side, my brother, Rusty, still slept, blanket wrapped tight around him on our opened-up sofa bed.

My dad yelled, "Linda!" I walked to the stairs and called up to my sister, calling louder until she answered.

She finally responded, irritated. "What?!"

"Daddy wants ya." As I turned back to the hall that led to the kitchen and my dad's room, my mom ran past me. That surprised me—not her running by me, her presence. A couple of months earlier Dad had kicked Mom out. Over her shoulder, she yelled, "Come on!" and she went out the back door. Then her new boyfriend, Jerry, running too, followed my mom right past me and out the door.

Moments later, my dad came out of the bedroom, blood all over his face, his shotgun in his hand, and left. Linda, at sixteen a fragile, pale beauty, came downstairs, wide awake. Rusty, age nine, woke up. I was already bawling, and he joined me. The three of us ran out our back door, yelling and squalling, into our yard. The commotion woke our neighbor, Mrs. Kaiser, whose back door faced ours. She came out, talked briefly with Linda, and told us to come into her house. An arm wrapped around each of us kids, Linda guided us in to wait for our dad.

At the Kaisers' house, none of us said much. Rusty's crying subsided, but his eyes were big and round. Between my sobbing, my breath was coming in quick, shallow gasps. I was seven, and fear was already rooted in my life. In our house, fights between our parents were frequent.

My parents' fights meant screaming, throwing things, and hitting. We knew it would get ugly once my dad threw his coffee cup. Linda would guide Rusty and me into the living room. It often got loud enough the neighbor would call the police. Many times, Rusty and I would cry ourselves hoarse as our parents, who were supposed to be our protectors, hurt each other. Then the police would show up. Yep, that was our house. . . .

Mom loved to drink and loved attention. My dad worked second shift, so he wasn't home at night. When she still lived with us, Mom would take us to bars with her sometimes so "she wouldn't look bad" and then tell us to walk home in the dark so we would be there when Dad got home. She told us Dad was mean to her and told us to lie to protect her.

My two oldest sisters—Betty, twenty, and Carol, eighteen—were already out of the house; they'd both gotten married soon after graduating from high school. Betty had married the man who lived next door. She had babysat his kids for a time, and before you knew it, they were married.

We waited for my dad for hours at Mrs. Kaiser's house. While it was still dark out, my dad, his eyes steely and his mouth set in a hard line, came to take us home. He was angry that we'd been at the Kaisers' place, that our "nosy neighbors" would be all up in our business, and he was restless, still wanting to find our mom and Jerry. As Linda tried to calm him down, Rusty asked, "Dad, if you kill them, what will happen to us?" Dad didn't really answer and motioned to get us to leave the safety of the Kaiser home.

I begged my dad to let me stay at the Kaisers'—I was too scared to leave. Mrs. Kaiser assured my dad that was okay with her, so I spent the night on her living room couch.

Linda told us later my dad had been asleep when my mom and Jerry came in the bedroom and said they wanted to talk like adults. My dad had gotten up and was putting on his pants, but Jerry, an amateur boxer, began hitting him in the face, breaking his nose. My dad picked up the loaded shotgun he kept near the bed, but in the struggle with Jerry he dropped the gun. We always figured

6

if he hadn't dropped that gun my mom and Jerry wouldn't have made it out of the house. My dad had gone through the bus station, train station, and airport looking for them—face bloodied, shotgun in hand.

For months, convinced they would return, Dad would stay up at night, waiting. I remember going downstairs to use the bathroom and I would hear the double click of the shotgun shell going into the chamber—"is that you, Donna?"

Sometime after my mom moved out, my dad, not one for a lot of words, announced they were getting a divorce, and matter-of-factly asked me, "Who do you want to live with, Mom or me?"

"Mom," I answered, just thinking of how pretty she was. My brother chose our dad. But a couple of nights later, my dad simply hollered upstairs, "Donna, you're living with me. Your mom don't want ya." Now my fear had a friend—rejection.

My parents' divorce was final in 1966. Back then, it was rare for the father to get custody. Completing the splintering of our family, Linda had married—like her sisters, right out of high school—and moved out. With Linda gone, my dad needed someone to stay with us when he worked. Almost immediately the woman that would become my stepmother entered. Her name was Betty, but we nicknamed her Dragon Lady. Someone told me she had been living in her car. She needed a place to stay, and Dad needed someone with us. For them, it was a win-win.

For me, life went from bad to worse. My mom was a drunk, but her attacks were all aimed at my dad. Now, however, I was the one experiencing the effects of my new stepmother's alcoholism: the sudden mood changes, horrible hangovers, and hallucinations.

When I told my dad about Betty, he just said, "You don't have to listen to her," and left for work. My brother would simply take off. And that left me. I saw a pattern I learned would repeat: my stepmom would be pleasant, running our home and going to her bookkeeping job—and then she'd get fired. She would get mad, leave for days, and then come back. I was the one being the adult, doing the cooking, cleaning, and ironing. But I was nine years old.

I never felt like I could take a full breath at our house. I never knew when my stepmom was going to go off again. In fact, at times I broke into hives as soon as I walked through our door. One time, my stepmom gave me permission to go to a friend's house, but when I came back just a few hours later, she had forgotten she'd given me permission, and she grounded me. Even then I noticed that though Dragon Lady forgot plenty of things, she always remembered I was grounded.

Betty also had the ability to work Dad up so much that he would take it out on us. We were guilty until proven innocent. Discipline was a belt from Dad or a switch from her (we had to pick) that always broke the skin and left bruises. I can remember my dad putting me in the tub to soak and saying he was sorry. I don't even remember what I did, but I was convinced I deserved it. It wasn't until I had kids of my own that I realized I hadn't deserved that awful abuse. I came to understand that those who were supposed to protect me either couldn't or simply didn't.

My mother had visitation privileges, but they didn't last long. I remember going to a pizza place in the neighborhood with her and her new guy, my soon-to-be stepdad, Jim. They both had had plenty to drink, apparently. We left the restaurant to go home, and Jim headed out, driving on the wrong side of the road! My sister Betty happened to be at the same pizza place, witnessed it all, and let my dad know.

Soon after that, Mom showed up and called my stepmother out of the house to fight. Maybe it was because she'd lost visitation or maybe it was just that Dragon Lady was there. It was dark so I couldn't see what was happening, but I could hear them, screaming at each other in the street right in front of our house. Someone called the police. Again.

My mom was pretty much out of the picture after that. I do remember my brother receiving birthday cards from her—with money! She rarely remembered my birthday, though. After a while, I didn't think about her much. If anyone asked about my mom, I would have to stop and think, "Wait—she's not dead; she lives right across the river."

In case you couldn't tell, I was not raised in a Christian home. I didn't even know what church was. About the same time my mom left, some kids moved in next door. They invited my brother and me to go to the Baptist church a few blocks away. No adults went with us. We were the ones running around in the balcony since we didn't know any better.

I'm thankful those kids invited us to church. Some wonderful people there began to guide and care for me. People like Mrs. Bandy and Mrs. Mabry, who were my first Sunday school teachers. They taught me how to behave. They taught me about Jesus and God, our Father. "He's like your dad," they would say. They never dreamt what that meant to me. My dad had a temper! My dad wasn't there to protect me! So, God was one more thing for me to fear.

I didn't know the love of God. I didn't know love, period. I certainly didn't know I could have a relationship with God. I believed He existed, but not there with me. I believed He could help me if He wanted to, but apparently, He didn't want to; I was basically on my own. I didn't know I could have a relationship with Jesus either and I don't remember hearing about Holy Spirit. It was a good ol' Baptist church and the Bible was the King James Version.

Six months after we started going to church, I watched my brother walk up front to give his life to Jesus, so I went because he did. I was baptized on Easter Sunday when I was nine. Later that same day, while I was in our dining room by myself, I heard a voice say, "Do you know what you did?"

Out loud, I repeated what the pastor had led me in saying: "I accept Jesus as my Savior in the name of the Father, Son, and Holy Ghost." Immediately, I felt a weight lift off my shoulders. And that is when my faith journey started.

I didn't understand until much later that God wanted to make sure I knew Him. He knew what I was going through—and would go through. Without Him, it would have ended much differently. He did not remove me from the situations, but He was with me. John 16:33 says, "I have told you all this so that you may have peace in me. Here on earth you will have many trials and sorrows. But take heart, because I have overcome the world."

Outside of the church and family, I didn't have many friends. Ironically, the same kids who invited me to church loved to get me in trouble. It started with, "Hey, say this word." Then we would all laugh. Next thing I knew, they went and told on me. It was true, I did say it, but so did they. I was the only one that got the belt or switch though. I was crushed. I trusted them! Rejection says that even friends will hurt you!

School wasn't a safe place either. I had buck teeth so bad I couldn't close my mouth. Kids made fun of me, pointed, and laughed at me. I couldn't get braces until I was fourteen and a high school freshman. But mine weren't like the braces kids wear today, often clear and nearly invisible. My braces were thick metal surrounding each tooth with very visible wires connecting them. Also, each day for a certain number of hours I had to wear headgear. Mine had a band around my head, another band intersecting that and going over my head, and a kind of metal "yoke" that came from the back on both sides to my mouth. I was able to go to school without the headgear, but as soon as I got home my stepmom made me put it on. That meant when I went to some place like the laundromat, the headgear went too.

I was grateful to have braces but having to go to the laundromat with the headgear—that was horrible! I felt like a freak. I couldn't look people in the eye. I got my braces off shortly before my senior year. I was so self-conscious and insecure. I didn't experience prom—I would have been too scared to go even if I had been asked. By then I just wanted to be invisible. I had no self-confidence or self-worth. I felt defined by what others thought of me—or even what I feared they might think of me.

I remember when my fear of my stepmother turned to disgust and anger. At home, the dishwasher was me. We had one single sink, so I had to keep emptying the dirty water and refilling the sink. If my stepmother found one dish, glass, or fork dirty, she would empty the cabinets and make me wash everything in them. One evening when I was fifteen, I was still washing the dishes and Dragon Lady started picking up the ones I'd done, scowling and turning them this way and that. She found a dish with a bit of grease on it, dropped it back in my soapy water, and without a word, opened the cabinets and began to take out the stack of dinner plates.

At that moment, I was washing a butcher knife. It would have been so easy to use that knife on her if I had not known who God was. I could hear a voice telling me not to do it. My fear of Him was so much greater than my hate for her. I put the knife down in the sink. Though I didn't realize it then, this was the first of many times God's voice directed my path.

John's Testimony

"Louisville? Louisville, Kentucky? We're moving again!? Are you kidding me!?"

At my outburst, my dad looked steadily at me, his brown eyes soft with patience and understanding. After fifteen years as a youth minister and now over two as a pastor, he was used to absorbing attacks from people. And as a man in ministry, he was used to moving—a lot.

I was in the middle of my sophomore year of high school. We had lived in San Antonio for almost three years, and my friends at school and church were important to me. We had moved five times since I was born in 1979, and I just wasn't ready to move again.

I thought I was pretty used to it—the cutting off of all my friendships; the letting go of toys, mementos, and belongings deemed not worth taking; the fuss of packing and unpacking; the strangeness of a new town, and new house; being the new kid at school, the one who didn't know anyone. And then reaching out and beginning to form new friendships.

Here I had some good friends at school, and even closer friends in my church youth group. We played sports, volunteered, went to concerts, and studied the Bible together. We were just starting to feel like a team. How was I supposed to pack up and leave them?

It didn't occur to me to talk to God about the move, or to pray that we wouldn't move. Although both my dad and mom were deeply spiritual, at this point in my life God and Jesus were just something I read about and heard about.

I was born in Beloit, Wisconsin, where my dad was serving at a Lutheran church as youth minister and minister of evangelism. I was baptized in the chapel of the hospital the same day I was born.

I've attended church my entire life and it pains my dad when I say this, but even through confirmation in the Lutheran church, I didn't fully allow God into my heart. I had book knowledge and I knew Jesus was my Lord and Savior, but I didn't have the relationship I do today with Holy Spirit. (For those wondering, I didn't forget "the" in front of Holy Spirit. Calling Him Holy Spirit is more relational to me, just like we say God or Jesus.)

Back then, when I heard we were moving again, it didn't occur to me, a fifteen-year-old kid who was all about me, how God had taken care of me my entire life or to trust that He would continue.

To say I was blessed is a drastic understatement. I was raised in a loving Christian home and my childhood was everything anyone could ask for. We never had a lot of money, but we always had food on the table. And though our parents couldn't afford on their own to take us on retreats or to amusement parks, because my dad was the youth leader and my mom his helper, my brother and I often got to go along. No matter what my dad's ministry role was, he was always a true leader who cut to the heart of things. My family was always welcomed by the churches where my dad served. I was welcomed.

When my dad was a youth minister, I often heard teens' parents thank my dad for his impact on their kids. One day my dad saw a couple of the young teen boys in his youth group picking on another kid. Two boys were holding the kid upside down. My dad walked in and said, "What in the hell is going on here?" They knew he was the new youth minister, and they immediately helped the guy up. My dad looked at Dan, who had been the instigator, and told him, "You're a leader. This isn't what leaders do." Dan went on to lead that youth group; he still gathers the members of the group for an annual reunion. And that kid that was turned upside down? He's now a pastor and my parents had the privilege of being at his ordination and installation.

I was used to hearing stories like this. And my mom—one of the nicest people you could meet, was always doing something for someone, whether it was my brother and me, someone at church, or a neighbor. She was the listening ear the teen girls in the youth groups sought out and privately confided in. During a difficult financial time for Dad's church, she "retired" from her position as church secretary but kept doing the same work—as a volunteer. She would watch other people's kids for free to give them a date night. She'd help clean and set up for church.

I joked that she'd do anything for anyone. Once, as an adult, I was lying on the couch and asked if she would take my contacts out. I wasn't serious—but my mom, a small frown creasing her forehead, got up, and moving toward me, softly said, "Well, I don't know how, but I'll try."

Awesome parents, right?

When I think about childhood baggage and hear about stories of abuse like Donna's, I feel petty bringing up having to deal with moving a lot. Sure, it was always awkward those first few days being the new kid. But I was blessed that people went out of their way to make friends with me because I was the new youth minister's (or pastor's) son.

However, there is no denying that all the moves had a major impact on my life. Because I had to deal with leaving friends so many times, I struggled to develop the deep relationships I saw among other guys. My defense mechanism to deal with relocating was to move on quickly and not think about the friends I had just left. I became distant in relationships—even with God. And I developed an underlying anger, anger that would surface suddenly.

I first remember it in my teenage years.

I was extremely competitive and didn't like to lose. On the ball field, I'd throw down my hat or hit the ground. A couple of months after we moved to Louisville, toward the end of my sophomore year of high school, I started

12

dating a girl. Soon after, one of the guys at school, a football player named Pee-wee, began giving me a hard time. He liked her, too, and she had turned him down shortly before we started dating. One day at school Pee-wee and I had some words in the hallway. We agreed to meet up after school to fight, thinking we wouldn't get in trouble.

I went to the agreed-upon spot, a store parking lot a couple of blocks from our high school. Pee-wee never showed.

That night I told my parents what had happened. They were disappointed. "Nothing anyone says to you is worth fighting," my dad said. They made me promise I wouldn't fight at school.

Well, not ten minutes after I walked in the next morning I saw Pee-wee in the hallway. I was going to ignore him, but after I passed him, I heard him call me a cuss word I wouldn't put in this book. I turned and said, "I showed up. You didn't." Suddenly, he lowered his head like a bull and came charging at me. I picked him up and body-slammed him. I jumped on his back and started punching him. Almost immediately two senior guys broke up the fight and a teacher came around the corner. The principal told my parents that it was the first fight he'd ever heard about between two honor students. He suspended us both for three days. A few days after returning to school, that girl broke up with me anyway. Pretty stupid.

My anger issues weren't over-the-top crazy, but they were a kind of baggage I would carry for many years to come.

Self-Reflection

Good or bad, our childhoods have a dramatic effect on our faith journey. For example, our view of our earthly fathers can skew our view of our heavenly Father. If your father was distant, or you didn't know your father, you have probably at some point viewed God as distant or non-existent. If your father was strict, you may have focused on God's laws and His judgment. If your father was loving and accepting, you likely see God that way. Regardless of how you view your earthly father, we can joyfully tell you that we all have a loving heavenly Father. First John 3:1a says, "See how very much our Father loves us, for he calls us his children, and that is what we are!"

It's important to deal with baggage caused by our childhoods. Our prayer is by our being transparent with our stories, you will spend time with God and ask for healing from any wounds from your childhoods.

- What were the defining moments, issues, or events of your childhood?

- From these, what observations or decisions did you make about life? People? Yourself?

- In your childhood, what was your relationship with God? Did you believe God existed? How did you view God?

*People who conceal their sins will not
prosper, but if they confess and turn from
them, they will receive mercy.*

—Proverbs 28:13

Chapter 2

YOUNG ADULT MISTAKES

John's Testimony

"**Y**ou're not going to like what happens if you hit me one more time," I said to Crystal. That was the second time she had smacked me in the face with her piece of string cheese. She thought it was funny. It certainly didn't hurt—it was string cheese!—but the anger that had been growing in my heart over the past year toward her was bubbling over. Sure enough, Smack!

I was eating an apple, and as Crystal laughed and turned back toward me, I threw it at her with all the force I had. It hit her right in the face. As bad as that was, I was so filled with anger that as the apple rolled back to me, I picked it up and started eating it again instead of making sure my wife was okay.

We were sitting at the kitchen table at our home with another couple, our friends Jeff and Christy. The shock and anger in Jeff's face brought me back to reality. I felt a wave of regret and embarrassment. My marriage had its issues, but never had my anger gotten physical until this moment. After Jeff's immediate rebuke and recognizing that what I had just done was inexcusable, I'm ashamed to say that my thoughts went to whether makeup would be able to cover the black eye that was forming. I certainly didn't want people at church to see Crystal like that the next day. How had our marriage come to this point?

Crystal and I had started dating near the end of my sophomore year in high school. She was my first serious girlfriend, and we became sexually active quickly.

In the middle of my senior year, when I learned my dad had a call to another church, I had several reasons for wanting to stay in Louisville. I had already started thinking about proposing to Crystal, and I'd been accepted to the University of Louisville. I could see opportunities where I was working—to get into sales, and maybe become a manager. At church, I was starting to help lead our youth group. I felt I was finally in the place I could plant some roots.

I was eighteen and don't recall my parents trying to change my mind. I had a plan for college, work, and a church home. I'm sure they had some reservations about moving away from me, but they did not put any pressure on me to move with them. They would only be 250 miles away. My brother is three years younger than I am; if he was going to miss having his big brother around, he didn't say it. If I thought about him at all then (remember, I was eighteen and all about me), I figured he was likely looking forward to being the only child in the house.

Not having a place of my own, I got the great idea of renting a room at Crystal's parents' house. I didn't even investigate any other options. I told myself—and my parents—it was economical and would help my girlfriend's parents. My dad warned me about the dangers, but I wasn't listening. I certainly wasn't paying attention to Proverbs 23:22a, "Listen to your father, who gave you life (NIV)."

It wasn't long before I realized moving into Crystal's house was a mistake. Her mom was giving me ultimatums in letter form: "If you don't keep the stairs to the second floor cleared, I will raise your rent." "Keep your room clean or I'll raise your rent." I was happy to help around the house and didn't react to that approach very well. It was also a drastic difference from living with my parents to essentially living with my landlord. In fairness to Crystal's mom, my mom had spoiled my brother and me. She would make whatever we wanted for dinner, iron our shirts, do our laundry; if we needed a notebook or calculator for school, she'd run right out and get it for us.

After only six months I was ready to move out and my now fiancé wanted to go with me. In my warped sense of right and wrong, I felt if we were going to move out on our own together, we should be married. We had talked about waiting for the wedding until we graduated from college, but instead, we moved up the date and got married just before we both turned nineteen.

Some young people are ready for marriage; I was not. I was extremely selfish. For the next few years, I was going to school full-time, working a full-time job, actively participating at church, and I spent every Saturday morning and sometimes other days with the guys playing basketball. I had become a social drinker who didn't think you could have a party without alcohol. I thought I was a good Christian because I went to church every Sunday, even if it did happen to be with a hangover.

Our marriage had problems. I was judgmental, jealous, controlling, and I focused on what she was doing that I didn't like. I zeroed in on her sins to justify mine. I prayed for a way out. How horrible is that? Instead of praying *for* my wife, *for* our marriage, and for God to *change me*, I was praying for a way to get out without feeling guilty.

We both made mistakes. I'm not going to talk about hers.

We tried counseling individually and together for three years but ultimately, we divorced after five years of marriage. I believed I had done everything I could to save the marriage and it wasn't meant to be. I even told people I was getting a guilt-free divorce.

We had been separated (working different shifts and frequently sleeping in different rooms) for over a year. We didn't have kids, didn't have many possessions, and by that point, we were both done and ready to move on separately. We sat at the kitchen table, divided up the bills and the few things we had, submitted everything to a lawyer, and, two weeks later, the divorce was final.

Little did I know the baggage from my first marriage would cause problems for years to come. I came out of that marriage much more afraid to trust. I became quick to feel jealousy and then anger. While I did tell Crystal, I was sorry for my mistakes, I didn't really mean it. It took many years for both of us to truly apologize and forgive.

After moving so many times, I had gotten used to cutting ties. To me, it seemed natural to be married with an extended family one day, and the next day completely shut off that part of my life. It's painful to me to think how hard-hearted I was.

Despite all my rationalizations, I knew God's plan for marriage. God did not cause or help me get a divorce. The Bible is straightforward on marriage.

Mark 10:9 says, "Therefore what God has joined together, let no one separate (NIV)." God will not tell us to do something contrary to His Word.

I was hesitant to share this part of my testimony. I'm not proud of these details. I don't want to glamorize divorce or draw any negative thoughts from anyone toward my ex-wife. However, I think opening the dark parts of my story will help some people. Perhaps you have been through a divorce and still have guilt, anger, or unforgiveness. God doesn't want us to live that way. John 10:10b says, "My purpose is to give them a rich and satisfying life."

Donna's Testimony

"Don't do it!" I heard God's familiar voice say. It was July 23, 1983. My wedding day.

I panicked! I could feel the walls caving in on me. I was twenty-five, and my husband was ten years older—with two kids not that much younger than me, and one of them a rebellious teenage boy. But everything was already paid for. My sisters had their dresses, the guys their tuxes, and everyone was expecting a wedding to happen in just a few hours. I felt like I couldn't turn back, and I told God it would be okay; *I would make it work.*

The wedding continued as planned. I hadn't invited my mom; in the years after she'd moved out, I'd tried to reach out to her, but when I had called, she didn't answer. And when I had stopped by her house, she rarely answered the door, even though I could see that she was home. When I had asked my dad about inviting her to my wedding, he said, "I'd rather be in a room full of snakes!" That was good enough for me—I was okay with that. When Mom found out I was married and hadn't invited her, she made sure I knew how hurt she was. I was okay with that too.

Soon after the wedding, challenges began to pile up: My husband's teenage son came to live with us. He wasn't out of line with me, but he and his dad argued a lot—I could hear them yelling and getting physical. That brought me right back to being seven again, with no control over what was happening. My heart would race, my stomach would clench—all that panic feeling would come over me.

Just a few months after the wedding, my dad, who'd had two heart attacks several years earlier, had a brain aneurysm that took his peripheral vision away and changed his personality—he became more emotional. In conversations, he would now respond with laughter, tears, or both. I could see that he loved us; he just had never known how to show it before.

Dad spent the last three months of his life in the hospital. During this time he was confused, so we—my stepmom, my sisters and I—all took shifts so someone was with him 24/7. I couldn't work full time because I was at the hospital so much. It was hard. He would get disoriented and try to get out of bed; or he'd give me a look that said, "You can't tell me what to do," and he'd start pulling out tubes. He'd say to me, "I might not be here when you get back." I was the only one he told that. Not my sisters or my brother, just me!

Maybe he was trying to prepare me for his death, but I was a mess. I would just kind of make a joke about it like, "Why, where do you think you're going?" Of course, I knew what he was talking about which put more stress on me even though that wasn't what he intended. I felt like I wouldn't have been able to live with myself if I wasn't there when he died. Besides, things were so uncomfortable at my house it felt like a relief to be with him. It was my safe haven.

I watched him take his last breath around 11:00 p.m. on April 6, 1984. That was the hardest thing I had ever been through. I couldn't believe I wouldn't see him anymore. For months afterward, my heart would stop every time the phone rang. It took me back to the numerous times I had been awakened and called to the hospital about Dad.

During this time, I was working and going to school at night. I had just been accepted to Louisville's Bellarmine University to finish my degree when the company I was working for laid off my entire division. Within two months I lost both my dad and my job.

I was so insecure at that stage of my life. I reacted to situations like I was still seven years old. It wasn't only my husband and stepson arguing that would trigger my emotions. If I heard strangers arguing on the street, I would panic; I had to get away from there. If someone was laughing, they were laughing at me. I resisted trying anything new; I was sure people would make fun of me. I cut myself out of so many things because I believed the lies in my head. I wanted to be loved but made bad choices trying to feel loved. I didn't have a positive example of how to be a wife, a mother, or even a friend. Life was unsettled at home, and I was in way over my head. I had learned when the going gets tough you run; so, I ran! After a year of separation, I filed for divorce.

Out of all that terrible time of loss, two wonderful things happened. One involved my dad. My dad had grown up Catholic, but after he married my stepmother, the church wouldn't allow him to take communion, so he left the Catholic Church. But my Baptist pastor visited him in the hospital and helped him realize that Jesus could heal the hurt my dad had experienced. My dad truly understood and received Jesus in his heart. I know he is in heaven!

The other was my relationship with my stepmom. She and I actually became friends. Shortly before Dad died, she stopped drinking and became a completely different person. She opened up to me about her life, including her relationship with her harsh father. She said he'd been hot-tempered, strict, and rigidly religious. For example, as a little girl, she had received the game Old Maid as a gift at school and brought the deck of cards home. Her dad had hit her with his belt and screamed at her, shaming her for "gambling."

She had started drinking in her teens, becoming an alcoholic, and her own mother had ended up raising my stepmom's two daughters. Maybe she was trying to make up for that by raising us. She had no idea of the scars I carried because of her, and neither did I for a long, long time.

I met my second husband at my sister Linda's house while he was helping build her privacy fence. I was twenty-nine and he was twenty-four. I thought he was the best thing that had ever happened to me. I loved him unconditionally; he was my best friend; he was my world. However, I was afraid I didn't deserve him. I didn't want to do anything to upset him or give him an excuse to leave me. I tried to be everything I thought he wanted me to be. He had no idea, of course, because I couldn't speak it out loud. He didn't know all the baggage I carried, and he wouldn't have understood. He had had a great childhood and his family was delightful—they got along well with each other and warmly welcomed me. I fell in love with them. His mom was a wonderful example for me, and I was as close to his sisters as I was to my own. We dated for about two and a half years before we got married. I was a nervous wreck. I was afraid he would change his mind and leave me at the altar. How crazy is that!?

Self-Reflection

Everyone makes mistakes. With mistakes come pain. We can stuff the pain down, do everything we can to ignore the pain, or we can heal the pain. If you're going to heal it, you must let the pain go.

Even if we learn from our mistakes, we sometimes carry away from our experience baggage that can hurt our future relationships. What do we mean by baggage? If someone hurts us, we may have difficulty trusting others, especially in the same type of relationship. If we had a harsh or abusive parent, we may rebel against authority figures.

To heal this baggage, first acknowledge it's there. Can you talk to others about your mistakes? If not, we challenge you to ask God to help you dive into the root of the problem. Your testimony is not only about the successes. Explaining what you learned from your mistakes can help others.

Maybe your relationships are not what you would like them to be, but you aren't aware of any issues or baggage you may have that would prevent you from having healthy, loving relationships. If so, you have options. You might consider meeting with a Christian counselor, your pastor, or a trusted friend. Tell God you repent of your sins and ask Him to help you heal any issues you have from past relationships. As the apostle Paul says in 2 Corinthians 10:4, "The weapons we fight with are not the weapons of the world. On the contrary, they have divine power to demolish strongholds (NIV)."

- What were the defining moments, issues, or events of your young adult years?

- Are you aware of any baggage you need God to help heal? Write down any issues you are aware of at this time. How will you heal them— what is your plan? Write out your plan.

- How might you use what you've learned to help others?

I prayed for this child and the Lord has granted me what I asked of him.

—I Samuel 1:27 (NIV)

Chapter 3

PRECIOUS GIFTS FROM GOD

Donna's Testimony

Aftar all the hurts I'd endured from other children and teens, I always thought, "Why would I want kids?"

Until I was told I couldn't have kids.

At the age of twenty, I was diagnosed with endometriosis. For me, this meant pain so severe at times I couldn't stand, sit, or lie down. At that time, my doctor told me there was no treatment for endometriosis, so he told me when I was tired of the pain, he would remove everything, and I would be fine. Again, I heard that quiet voice inside, telling me not to listen. I thought about 1 Corinthians 6:19, which says, "Do you not know that your bodies are temples of the Holy Spirit, who is in you, whom you have received from God? You are not your own (NIV)." If it was God's will for me to have a child, I felt it would be a sin if I allowed the doctor to take away the option.

My young adult years were a time of challenges, and my fears still hampered me, but also brought precious gifts and miracles from God, and a deeper faith and relationship with Him. The endometriosis was one example. Through the pain, diagnosis, and my switch in attitude about having kids, I saw once again how God's timing is perfect but rarely ours. Although I had known I wanted children before my first marriage, I wasn't with the right person. Nor was I the person I needed to be. And at the time I had been diagnosed, the surgery to treat endometriosis wasn't even available.

I had been married to my second husband for about a year and a half when my sister Carol told me she had talked to her doctor about my endometriosis. There was a new procedure available—laser surgery—and he believed he could help me.

Naturally, as soon as I had the surgery, I expected to get pregnant immediately! There had been no chance before, but now the anticipation was overwhelming. I was praying and bargaining with God. I knew in my heart that my purpose was to be a mother. I felt like this child would be a boy and I would dedicate him to the Lord and raise him in church.

I also knew I had anger issues and no patience! I prayed God would help me to be the best mom I could be. In the end, I only had to wait three months, but that was ninety days of beating myself up. The funny thing is, I was almost three weeks past my normal cycle before I realized I was late.

I loved being pregnant! It was the best I had felt in my life. Tiring and nerve-racking, but also beautiful, especially when that life inside me started moving. I didn't tell anyone, other than family, until after the ultrasound at twenty weeks. I wanted to make sure everything was completely okay before I said anything.

And everything was okay until my eighth month when my doctor told me that my baby had stopped growing. He ran tests to see what was going on. I was supposed to get the results in about a week, but my baby decided not to wait. It was a Saturday evening and my husband and I were three hours out of town. My labor pains were about ten minutes apart when we started back home. Believe it or not, I was driving. But then my labor pains were coming faster and harder. We stopped at a rest area about halfway, and all heck broke loose. My water broke in the restroom, so I got in the back seat. White-knuckling the steering wheel, my husband drove, going pretty fast, hoping to attract a police officer to escort us. I was rocking back and forth, breathing with short puffs like the Lamaze class taught me. My pains were around two minutes apart when we got to the hospital about midnight. My husband asked if I wanted him to carry me. I said, "No, I'm here; I'm going in!"

Because I walked in on my own, the nurses at first didn't seem to take me seriously. They slowly took my information, had me wait for a wheelchair . . . maybe they figured I didn't understand what was going on; it was my first child, after all. Things changed quickly once they examined me and I mentioned, "Maybe you could check . . . when I saw the doctor a week ago, he said the baby was breech." I was now seven centimeters dilated and my baby was indeed positioned wrong—feet first instead of head first. A breech baby.

Bam! Now the nurses moved fast: they got me an operating room, brought in an anesthesiologist, put an IV line in my arm. My doctor was giving orders over the phone while driving to the hospital! By the time he got to me twenty minutes later, I was ten centimeters dilated and ready to go. I had planned for a natural, drug-free birth. But no, since my baby was breech, my doctor put me under and performed a C-section. James Codey was born three weeks early at 12:49 a.m. on Sunday, Feb 16, 1992. He was nineteen inches long but weighed only 4.8 pounds.

The nurse woke me up in the recovery room. I was so groggy. I felt like I had had a surgery but couldn't remember why. My husband was standing beside me, a small frown creasing his forehead. The doctor was off to the side, filling out paperwork. My husband said, "We have a boy!" His voice seemed thin. He stammered, "He . . . he's really little and has a . . . a—"

"She doesn't need to know that right now," the doctor interjected. I fell asleep wondering what in the world was wrong.

It was fourteen hours before I could see Codey for the first time. I don't do well with anesthesia, so I was reeling from nausea and brain fog. Doctors kept coming around putting papers in my face to sign. A nurse told me Codey was in the regular nursery. Then another nurse came and said they were moving him to NICU. The later it got, the more anxious I became. Eventually, someone brought me a polaroid picture to prove he was alive, but I couldn't go see him and they couldn't bring him to me. It turns out that around my seventh month he had contracted cytomegalovirus, a mild virus common in adults, but potentially deadly for fetuses. Codey had spent the rest of his time fighting that rather than developing and growing any bigger. He was also born with a cleft lip and palate. I didn't know what any of that meant. I just wanted to see my baby. I wanted to hold my baby boy.

I was finally able to go see Codey around two o'clock in the afternoon. My husband had tears in his eyes by the time we arrived at the NICU. I asked why, and he said, "I'm afraid you're not going to love him because he looks funny." He didn't understand; I had loved Codey long before he was born. Finally, I was able to hold him! He looked so pitiful: he had a tube in his nose, wires coming off his head, and an IV in his tiny arm. His little feet, bruised from all the needle sticks, looked like purple pincushions. But I saw him smile. At that moment I felt certain my dad was talking to him and watching over him from heaven.

Because I'd had a C-section, I was able to stay at the hospital a few extra days, but we still had to leave without our baby. Codey would be in NICU another twenty-one days. That's how long it took him to reach five pounds. God had already provided by blessing my husband with a good job and excellent insurance so we could give Codey the care he needed. God knew there would be several surgeries in Codey's future.

My husband worked third shift, leaving home at 10:30 p.m. and getting back around 8 a.m. This meant much of the time as I cared for Codey my husband was either sleeping or gone. As I recovered from the surgery, taking care of Codey occupied me 24/7. The nurse told us he was underdeveloped and needed to sleep at a forty-five-degree angle so he could breathe easier. I had him sleep in a baby swing. He cried if the swing stopped, so I would wake up every forty-five minutes or so and crank the swing up. Codey's lip was not attached, and he had no palate (roof of his mouth), which affected his ears and nose as well, so we had to learn how to feed him. He couldn't suck on a bottle, so we had to enlarge the hole on the nipple of the bottle and force the milk in his mouth. He had colic and reflux and would wake up at night like he was choking and couldn't get his breath. Finally, when he could breathe, he would scream.

One night, he started screaming and this time I couldn't calm him. I tried everything I knew to do. Nothing helped. I raised him up, looked him in the eyes, and yelled, "What do you want from me?!" At that moment, his cries went from "something is wrong" to fear. I saw fear in my own child! That moment changed my life. The fear I saw in him was the same fear I had as a child. I never wanted my children to have to be afraid of their parents like I was. From that point forward, God helped me with self-control and patience so that I would not react in anger like my parents did.

A friend asked me, "You prayed for patience, didn't you?"—as if that was the reason Codey was born with issues. I don't know about that, but I do know dealing with Codey and taking care of him taught me patience. I learned much more from Codey than I could ever teach him.

In the first year of Codey's life, he went through three surgeries. For his first surgery, to fix his cleft lip, he had to be ten pounds. He finally reached that at five months old. Yes, I said five months. His "newborn" clothes swallowed him when he was born. Just a month later he had surgery to fix a double hernia, and then again at ten months, to connect his cleft palate. His doctor didn't have to build up his palate, which was good, but after the surgery Codey still had no gag reflex and had difficulty swallowing and speaking. He would also need speech therapy when he got older. Each surgery was difficult for me as a new mom. I had to hand over Codey, in his little hospital gown with his big smile and bright eyes, to the nurse. And then wait. I could hardly breathe! The good news—once he was through the surgeries, he was a happy, healthy, beautiful blonde little boy!

Shortly after Codey's third surgery, my stepmother passed away. I took her death harder than I thought I would. She'd transformed her life: she had been faithfully attending church and had found her purpose volunteering for Red Cross. She had lived by herself since my dad had died.

One Sunday she didn't show up at church. My sister-in-law found her—she had the phone in her hand but never had the chance to use it. Maybe it was a stroke, maybe a heart attack, but it was sudden and unexpected. She'd told me once, "I'm afraid to die and I don't want to die alone." I felt so bad that her worst fear had come true.

At the time of my stepmother's death, I was pregnant with my second child. My doctor told me this pregnancy was considered high risk because of my age, and the issues my firstborn had had. So he ordered an amniocentesis at twenty-eight weeks. What an amazing experience! I was able to watch my baby respond to the needle that suddenly showed up. He looked right at the needle and raised up his little hand, his fingers starting to reach for it. The doctor said "No!" and tapped my tummy. My baby's hand jerked back, and he left the needle alone. At that moment, I witnessed his reactions. He could sense, hear, and feel emotions even though he was in the womb!

Labor pains woke me early one Sunday morning. They were five minutes apart! They remained five minutes apart for an hour so the doctor on call told me to go to the hospital. My oldest sister met us there to pick up Codey, and I think it was over by the time she got home. Just two hours and forty-five minutes from the first pain, John Casey arrived, perfectly formed and healthy, in a natural, drug-free delivery. Sunday, May 30, 1993, 6:17 a.m., seven pounds, three and a half ounces and twenty and a half inches long. I remember when I got to the labor and delivery room another mother in labor there was having a rough time; she was pretty loud. After I gave birth, as they rolled me out to take me to the recovery room, I could hear her saying, "She's done already! Are you kidding me!?"

I wasn't sure how Codey, then fifteen months old, was going to react when I brought Casey home. He hadn't been walking very long and was still behind most kids his age. I felt guilty, like I had done something wrong. He was used to all the attention and now he had to share. But I was relieved and delighted that Codey welcomed and loved Casey.

Casey was such a good baby. He only cried when he was hungry or tired. I went back to work part-time when he was three weeks old, and full-time when he was three months old.

My husband and I had started a multi-level marketing business before we found out I was pregnant with Codey. My plan was to continue to grow the business and work from home. Once Codey was born, my attention went completely to taking care of him, so the business slowed down drastically. I tried to pick it back up off and on for a couple of years, but I could never give it consistent focus. I would try to visit people on Saturdays and make it back before my husband had to leave for work early Sunday morning. That meant a lot of driving home in the middle of the night.

During those drives the Lord saved my life many times, building my trust in Him, and humbling and amazing me that He would work miracles—for *me*! Here are two.

The first time, I was making a late-night five-hour drive from Jonesville, Virginia, to my home in Louisville, Kentucky. At 3:30 in the morning, I was still an hour and a half away and the temperature was falling. It was raining but I didn't notice it freezing. I was on an overpass when the car swung almost sideways and was heading for the guardrail on the left. If you've had an experience like that, you understand how everything goes in slow motion. I was calm and knew I was probably going to die, and then that voice said, "Turn the wheel." I turned the wheel and my eyes closed. When I opened them, I was past the overpass right before a hill, off the road, facing the right direction and stuck in mud. There was a car behind me already stopped; the driver had gotten out and was walking toward me. At the same time, from the opposite direction, a police officer was pulling up.

When I got out of the car, I could hardly stand; the road was a solid sheet of ice. The officer told me there was a multi-car collision right over the hill and if this hadn't stopped me, I would've been part of it. I said, "I need to get home to my kids so my husband can leave for work."

The officer responded, "Nope. That's not gonna happen. You cannot drive any further." He escorted me down the exit, just yards away, right into the parking lot of the hotel at the bottom of the exit. When I got to the room, I could see the crash from my window!

The second time was in the afternoon after work. I had both boys in the car with me, still in car seats. I had just picked them up from the babysitter, and I was on the expressway, in the left lane, with construction and concrete dividers on both sides. Next thing I knew, I felt an ice-cold pressure on my left hand—between the thumb and forefinger—like someone was applying an ice cube to that patch of skin. It wasn't until that point I realized I had fallen asleep! Now wide awake and shaking, I kept looking down expecting to see someone holding ice to my hand. That sensation would not go away for another ten to fifteen minutes. We got home safely and I had no doubt we had been supernaturally delivered from what might have been a fatal accident.

I asked God for protection over my boys and to reveal to me what I needed to do and lead me to be aware when something wasn't right. And, thankfully, He did! Casey rarely got sick, but Codey regularly had ear infections and strep throat. Usually, when he had an ear infection, I knew immediately, because his ear would turn blood red and he would cry out in pain.

When the boys were two and three years old, I looked for a daycare for them close to my work—and a friend told me about one at a Catholic school right down the street. Their daycare accepted my flexible schedule, and I could get to Codey quickly when he needed me.

My fear took over a few years later when it came time to think about school. I couldn't allow myself to put Codey in public school. I knew what it was like to be made fun of, and I wanted to protect him as much as possible. Thankfully, the Catholic school where he attended daycare went up to eighth grade, so Codey had an easy transition into kindergarten, along with his friends. I know now that God had answered my fear by bringing that school into our lives. I knew that my faith, at that time, was not strong enough to give them the firm Christian foundation they needed. The Catholic school taught the love of Jesus and family values. They cared about the whole person. And I knew my boys were protected and safe. Coming from a Baptist background, I struggled with differences in doctrine, but was reassured that we all believed Jesus to be the Son of God.

Codey had more health crises after he turned five. He was on the couch one night near bedtime. When his dad pulled his shirt off over his head to get him ready for bed, Codey yelped. He said his neck hurt. His ears seemed fine, no fever. I couldn't see any reason for his pain. He slept fine, but the next morning he still said his neck hurt when he moved it, so I took him to the doctor. By the time we got there, a raised knot had appeared behind his ear. His doctor took one look and left the room. He came back about ten minutes later and told me he was making arrangements at the hospital and to take him there *now*. It turns out he had an infection *behind* the ear that could move into his brain. He remained in the hospital on IV antibiotics for three days. Once again, we thanked God for His protection!

Another time I came home from work and noticed Codey wasn't breathing normally. I asked him if he was feeling okay. He took a gulp of air, on the exhale said, "I'm fine," and took another gulp of air. He was talking and happy, like nothing was out of the ordinary. But I had that momma's sense about this. His doctor's office was already closed, and the immediate care clinic didn't see any reason to bring him in. Finally, they said if I really thought he was having trouble, take him to the hospital.

I walked in the emergency room with Codey and told the receptionist, "I know you're going to think I'm crazy, but he acts like he has emphysema!" The receptionist got the triage nurse, who came into the waiting room and lifted Codey's shirt. I was stunned. His belly curved deeply inward—it looked like his stomach was gone. The nurse said, "Let's go." I heard one gentleman fussing because his wife had been there for a while and was in pain. The nurse turned to him and said, "A child not breathing takes precedence, Sir." More staff appeared; they were taking us back and taking our information at the same time. They put him on the bed and started a breathing treatment. After everything calmed down, the doctor told me Codey could no longer use his normal chest muscles to breathe and was using his neck and stomach muscles to help him. He was having an asthma attack! I didn't know what that was. The doctor believed the asthma attack was triggered by allergies and that I should get him tested. We thanked God for protecting Codey until I could get him help!

I could see Codey was developing a strong connection with Jesus. One day Codey asked me how I got him. I told him I had prayed for him, and God gave him to me. Shortly after that, his teacher came to me. She said Codey had told her if she wanted a baby, all she had to do was ask and God would give her one. She told me she was pregnant at that time but didn't yet know.

After Codey's asthma attack, I set up allergy testing. The sticks on the back weren't bad—he didn't cry at all with them. But they also did both arms, each time poking the needle in, then using it to raise his skin for the injection. Forty times on each arm. Neither of us had expected that, and I cried right along with him. When I found out the results, it looked like he was allergic to everything living but me. The allergy doctor put him on several medicines plus shots. We were on our way to the first visit for shots when Codey asked me how many and how often. I didn't have the heart to tell him. I said we would find out when we got there. A couple of minutes later, he said, "Mom—Jesus told me I would get two shots, one in each arm, three days a week, but they won't hurt." He was right!

Not surprisingly, I was under a lot of stress. When I wasn't working, I was with my boys. I was so focused on taking care of them that I didn't realize my husband and I were headed in two different directions. By this time, we had been married about nine years. I had loved him so much that I was afraid to lose him, and then I did. So, after a "short" two-and half-year process, the divorce was final, and he moved out. I still believed that once we were separated for a while, he would realize how much he loved us and return. Instead, he moved on. My husband left and a part of me left with him. However, to this day I am thankful that God chose him to be their dad.

I hated that my boys were now a statistic, children of divorced parents, and history was repeating itself. I've had bouts of depression in my life, but this was the worst. I had to watch my husband move on with his life with someone else. Watch him bring another woman into the boys' lives. I couldn't eat. I couldn't sleep. I don't know how I took care of the boys during that time.

My life revolved around my boys, so depression would increase when they went to their dad's. I would sit at home and stare at the walls. Suddenly, I was afraid of being in the house by myself. I had forgotten what it was like to have that level of fear. I didn't feel safe or whole unless they were with me.

Going to my pastor for counseling led to an epiphany that changed my life. The pastor asked about my childhood. How in the world did that have anything to do with what was going on now? I told him a little about what it had been like growing up, including Dad's temper and the spankings I had received.

When he asked, "What did you do wrong?" I said I didn't really remember, but I'm sure I deserved them.

He said, "Aren't your boys about the same age you were?" And when I said yes, he asked me, "What could they do that you would spank them like that?" Wow! I hadn't seen that coming.

"I don't think there is anything," I answered slowly, thinking, ". . . I don't think there is anything they could do that would deserve that." He told me I was right, and there was nothing *I* could have done to deserve that either. This was some of the best wisdom I had received in my life.

By this time, I was a forty-three-year-old single mom with two small boys. Divorced for the second time. Even in this darkness, I knew God was there, still protecting us. I knew what it was like to live from check to check each month, and—you know the saying—too much month, not enough money. I remember praying I would get paid before the checks I was mailing hit the bank. I had been giving an offering ever since I could remember. However, I didn't understand the significance of tithing until then. Speaking about tithing in Malachi 3:10, God says, "Test me in this . . . and see if I will not throw open the floodgates of heaven and pour out so much blessing that there will not be room enough to store it (NIV)." God gave His promise to me! So I stepped out in faith and gave first. When tithing I've always had enough. I've even seen a check come, completely unexpected! I don't know how all this works, but I'll say that the more I have given Him my firsts in time, talents, and treasure, the more I have seen Him work with the rest. It is simply giving thanks to God and not giving and expecting something in return.

John's Testimony

"I feel blessed I didn't have kids in my first marriage." I've said that several times and I typically get one of two responses. First, "I completely understand." That usually comes from someone that has been through a divorce with children or has a blended family now. Or the second response is a question: "You don't like kids?"

That question stings a little. It's not that I don't like kids. But in my first marriage, I was young, wasn't ready, and had zero patience for anything that changed my plans.

I'd love to think I would have changed my ways if we had had kids, but it could have easily gone the other way. It's probably not theologically correct to say God prevented me from having children because He had other plans later for me, but the thought has crossed my mind.

Years later, I would be completely unprepared to deal with Donna's children.

Self-Reflection

Our young adult years are often a time of challenges but can also be used to deepen our faith and relationship with God. Add on having children under less than perfect conditions or dealing with not being able to have kids, and it's no wonder that many of us struggle with fully understanding God's love for us.

Regardless of the specific challenges you've faced, you have likely gotten past many of them. Being able to recognize the help and even miracles God used to get you through them is an important step in your faith journey.

We pray you see how much God loves you. God sent His Son, Jesus, fulfilling the law through His suffering, dying, and being resurrected to pay for our sins. To say He endured this "challenge" to restore our relationship with Him is an understatement. Our lives are changed forever when we can grasp just how much God loves us.

- What challenges have you faced in your early adult years and how has God shown up during those times?

- How has having kids, or not having kids, affected your understanding of God's love?

- What's one example when God's plan for your life wasn't what you expected or wanted at the time, but looking back, you are grateful for His plan?

Then the Lord God said, "It is not good for the man to be alone. I will make a helper who is just right for him."

—Genesis 2:18

Chapter 4

THE DATING GAME

John's Testimony

"You guys should go together," a coworker told Donna and me. The company we worked for had given all employees a movie ticket and dinner gift card, and we had both just revealed neither of us had plans for the coming Friday. I was twenty-four and only two weeks past my divorce being final. I certainly wasn't looking for a date, but dinner and a movie sounded pretty good. I didn't know Donna very well, but it was a free night out and better than sitting at home alone.

I asked, "Well, whaddya think?" and Donna said yes.

I wasn't sure how our conversation would go since I didn't know how much we had in common, but I wouldn't have to talk during the movie anyway. I did know Donna liked Baby Ruth candy bars, so I took one with me. It was November 14, 2003.

We went to dinner at a local steakhouse and—surprisingly—talking was easy. Donna spoke about her boys, and I could see the sparkle of a proud mother. I told her about the building project at my church and, of course, talked a bit about work. We even talked a little about football and basketball, two sports I follow. I was surprised that Donna stayed interested, asking questions about the games.

After the movie we talked in the parking lot. Only because Donna is a hugger did we hug at the end. When I hugged someone (which was rare), it always felt awkward, and I would rush to separate. Donna, on the other hand . . . people have always said what a wonderful hugger Donna is. Her hugs feel like a warm blanket of love. So—we hugged, it felt nice (I didn't pull away) and afterward we went our separate ways. As I drove away, I started wondering if there was something else there other than just being coworkers.

But back at work on Monday our coworkers started making some jokes. "How was your date with the cougar? What was it like going to the movies with your mom?" I didn't respond. I said to myself, "It wasn't a date." I know now that Donna was upset by their jokes. Then, though, she didn't show it. And our interaction at work didn't change; we were still just coworkers. A few days went by, however, and I kept thinking about that night. "*Was* it a date?"

A week or so later, I was driving to my parents' house for a four-day Thanksgiving visit and my phone rang. It was Donna! My heart started beating faster when I saw her name come across the screen. She asked if I had been thinking about our time together the previous week. We both thought there may be more to the relationship and decided we should start that weekend by emailing questions back and forth and getting to know each other better.

In our emails, we talked through all the reasons we shouldn't date. That started with our age difference. People are shocked when they hear we have a twenty-one-year age difference. (I bet you just looked at our picture on the back cover.) Our other reasons to not date: she had two kids; I had just gotten a divorce; we both had baggage, including trust issues; my dad was a Lutheran pastor—she was attending a Catholic church (and had grown up Baptist); we worked together; and the list went on. Ultimately, none of those reasons scared us.

These emails became quite an obsession for me over the next few weeks. We took turns asking a question and discovered we both enjoyed the humor of our silly and creative subject lines, like, "Think Low Expectations, Then Go Lower"; "Mr. Notperfect"; "Full Steam Ahead"; "Whatever, Dude"; "I'm Clueless"; and "Hit the Road, Jack." Donna had responsibilities with her boys so her emails would usually come late. I was so eager to hear from her I would go to sleep but set my alarm for 11:00 p.m. and see if she had sent anything.

In addition to the emails, over the next few weeks we went out several times (actual dates!) and I was ready to take the relationship further by meeting her friends and family. It was Christmas Eve, and the boys were with their dad, but the rest of her family gathered at Donna's house. She wasn't prepared to let me come, and I respected her decision. I wanted to see her for Christmas, though, so she said she would let me know when the party was over and everyone had left.

I figured they would be gone by 10:00 p.m. and it was a bit of a drive to get to her place, so I drove over and parked down the street. She had no idea I was there. Some might say I had stalker tendencies; I say I was just excited to see her. I ended up falling asleep in the car. She eventually called around 11:00 and apologized that it was so late. To her surprise, I said I was down the street waiting.

A few months later, I met her boys, Codey and Casey, and the rest of her family and friends. It didn't take long after that to know she was the one. But since my divorce was so recent, my plan was to take some time before dating. I was asking God for direction and guidance. I needed to figure out what my priorities in life were and figured a relationship would just complicate that.

However, God had other plans.

I found myself irresistibly attracted to Donna. She has big brown eyes, wavy brown hair, and a wide, quick smile, along with a slim figure and graceful movement. But the attraction wasn't just physical. She has a joy people (definitely including me) just want to be around. She deeply loves and respects God. If you look up *people-person* in the dictionary, you'll see Donna's picture there. She loves family—being with them, talking with them, keeping in touch. Her positive outlook lifts my spirits and encourages me, and she brightens up the room while not having to be the center of attention. With Donna, my need to distance and my trust issues melted away; Donna acted in ways I had not experienced with any girlfriend. For example, she lifted me up to be the leader in the family and supported what I said. And other times, rather than erupt at me in front of other people, she would wait and tell me privately how what'd I'd said or done caused her to feel and what she wanted from me. I felt—and feel—respected and appreciated. I couldn't spend enough time with her.

I planned to propose to Donna at Ruth Chris' on the one-year anniversary of our first date since the restaurant had an outside balcony that would be the perfect spot. The only problem was it was about twenty degrees that night. Still, I was determined to stick to my plan. I was, and still can be, very stubborn. I gave her the speech I'd planned and rehearsed, and, thankfully, she still said yes. She may have just said yes to get out of the cold, but I took it.

Donna's Testimony

I had heard someone talk about writing a letter to God about what she wanted in a husband, so I decided to write one too. He had to be a Christian. I wanted a godly man that would be the head of the house, who didn't have children of his own but would accept mine, and who would love me unconditionally and accept me for who I am. I didn't want to pretend to be someone I wasn't just to be loved.

I also didn't believe there was anyone out there that would fit that description.

When John and I decided to go out that Friday night, I wasn't looking forward to it. My feelings were in turmoil. Although I wanted to be in a relationship and get married, I'd experienced so much hurt I was afraid to try again. But I was happy at the idea of just being with someone—at that point in my life I always felt scared at home by myself. Then again, I worried that we'd have long, awkward silences, since any time someone asked John a question at work, all I heard were one-word answers.

His thoughtfulness in bringing my favorite candy bar surprised and delighted me. I enjoyed our conversation, which flowed easily and comfortably. John was attentive, listening closely and asking interested questions. His corny humor kept me laughing. I relaxed.

That all changed back at work Monday. I took seriously our coworkers' jokes. I felt like a high school kid again, certain that others were making fun of me and laughing at me. Like John said, there were issues and a lot of obstacles between us. I had put up a wall to protect myself. I didn't want to trust anyone again.

And yet, I couldn't stop thinking of John. And it felt like God was encouraging me, "Go ahead, you won't be hurt this time." So I called. And we talked.

John was understanding. Nothing I said discouraged him, not my age, not my kids, not my divorces. Nothing.

My biggest hurdle was age. It hadn't occurred to me to mention age in my prayer! I didn't know the man God had for me would be two decades younger than me, but there we were—and here we are—in this unconventional relationship. It certainly proves God does have a sense of humor. I was afraid of meeting John's friends and family or introducing him to mine. How would *they* respond to our age difference? I had never heard the word *cougar* and I was mortified at the idea that some people might think of me as a *cougar*, but eventually, I stopped thinking about our age difference. That was because of John. He kept telling me, "Age is just a number. It doesn't matter." He called himself an "old soul." And that seemed true—in lots of ways I was more familiar with current trends, like music, than he was.

Even now, our age difference never seems to be an issue until someone asks for our ID's. Then I brace myself for the reaction.

Still, I continued to be anxious over our relationship: I didn't want my boys to become attached to someone only to have him leave. However, John's consistent openness and encouragement gradually overcame my fears. I learned that John wore his heart on his sleeve—I didn't have to guess what he was thinking. I could be honest and tell him what I thought, good, bad, or ugly, and we could talk through it. He didn't run or get defensive. If we disagreed, I could explain my side and he'd usually understand and accept.

Eventually, I told my family about John and told them all the obstacles we were struggling with. I discovered they didn't care about any of that, as long as I was happy. My walls slowly came down. I certainly understood that his parents would be unsettled about us as well. In fact, when we met with his parents to say we were engaged, I felt under fire as John's dad questioned me. His battery of questions included stuff like, "What were the causes of your divorce?" And when I told him, he said, "That's not necessarily reason to divorce." He seemed so judgmental to me. But he shared some stories that gave us hope, and he did say our marriage could work as long as Christ was in the center. (And I'm happy to say that John's dad's perspective has changed; in fact, he tells us he's used our relationship in sermons and in counseling as an example of success.)

Putting Christ at the center . . . that was one priority we made where we were better together. John pushed us to go to church as a family and be active in church. And he says about me, "Donna made sure we prayed daily, before meals and with her boys before bed." It took time, but we learned over and over that our happiness comes not from our partner but from our relationship with Christ.

I felt like God had brought John to me at just the right time. Everything seemed to fall into place.

One other thing—about that proposal. . . . Of all the times John has been romantic, the proposal wasn't one of them. It really did feel rehearsed as he kind of stiffly talked about being committed to me and my boys. It wasn't really a surprise; we had already talked about the ring. And it wasn't just cold, it was *freezing*. Granted, it was a beautiful night: we had a view of most of the city and the stars were bright in the clear sky.

I was glad he was that committed, and a quick yes did get me back inside the restaurant.

Self-Reflection

Dating can be complicated. From finding someone, to knowing what to do, to finding the *right* person. We've heard countless testimonies of God's bringing people together that weren't looking for each other. For those that are currently single, we might suggest the following: 1. Know God and talk to Him often; 2. Know yourself—how do you need to change to be more like Christ? Commit to do that; and 3. Know you deserve a partner that looks to God first and treats you with honor and respect.

Because God has a sense of humor, we might also add a fourth: Be careful what you pray for.

- If you are single, do you have a clear idea of the traits you are looking for in your ideal mate? Consider writing them out. Are they pleasing to God? What does the Bible say you should look for?

- What are a few key ways you need to change to be more like Christ? Commit to do that.

- What is, or what do you expect to be, the role of your Christian faith in your marriage? How do you prioritize your relationship with Jesus and your spouse?

If we claim we have no sin, we are only fooling ourselves and not living in the truth.

—I John 1:8

Chapter 5

RATIONALIZING WITH GOD

John's Testimony

"Let's move in together," I told Donna. Although I was a Christian, I was used to rationalizing to avoid submitting to God. I told myself it was logical, simple: We selected a wedding date in the summer to align with good dates for the honeymoon. (We saved a vacation day by picking a holiday week). We both owned a house and had two sets of bills, so it only made sense to move in together to save money. I also rationalized that marriage wasn't a piece of paper; it was a commitment that two people made together in front of God. With that definition, we were already married anyway.

I know now this was a bad decision. My rationalization doesn't change what is written in Scripture. Hebrews 13:4 says, "Marriage should be honored by all, and the marriage bed kept pure, for God will judge the adulterer and all the sexually immoral (NIV)." My decision was a horrible example to set for our sons. This has turned into a sin they have fallen prey to as well.

Years later, Donna told me she wasn't comfortable doing this at the time but felt pressured by me. Even to this day, I can be pushy, but thankfully she will now tell me exactly what she's thinking. More importantly, she'll tell me what she's hearing from God.

Neither of us wanted the expense of a big wedding, so we limited the number of people we invited. The wedding and reception were in our backyard. My dad, who presided over the ceremony, required that we go through pre-marriage counseling (for which I am grateful). The counselor took issues Donna and I had already talked about and helped us dive deeper into them and develop a plan for them. For example, saying it would be smoother for us as a blended family, our counselor advised us to have Donna be the chief disciplinarian. That was a hard one for me, but as challenges came up—and oh boy, did they ever—it helped that we could keep going back to what the counselor had said.

My bachelor party is one of the strangest you'll hear about. It was a small group, with me by far the youngest. It included my father (a Lutheran pastor), and several friends with a range of faith views: a Rastafarian, a friend I called a denominational mutt (he attended many kinds of churches over the years), and a few lifelong Catholics. Our bachelor party activity? We closed a bar while discussing various theological differences, covering topics from baptism to communion to purgatory. No telling what the bartender was thinking, but one thing I've learned is when you share about God, someone you may not have noticed is often listening. Sometimes they will engage and other times it may just be one of many seeds planted in their hearts that will bloom later.

The next morning, I handled setting up for the wedding and reception. Throughout the planning phase, I kept a list of everything needing to be done and rehashed it numerous times with Donna. She's told some people that her favorite part of our wedding day was the List Burning Ceremony. Yes, we literally set the to-do list on fire.

When I look back on our early to mid-years of marriage, I'm not sure how Donna made it. Sure, our life together was wonderful in many ways—we were active members at a local Catholic church; we volunteered at numerous events; we had great friends; we argued but made up quickly and never threatened divorce. But in truth, I was Donna's third child to raise. I was still selfish, judgmental, jealous, controlling, and had a bad temper.

The boys were in the fourth and fifth grade when Donna and I started dating. I never wanted or expected to replace their dad. He was still in the picture and loved them very much. To the boys' credit, I never once heard them tell me, "You're not my dad." They were always respectful.

I think the world of my parents and they did a great job raising my brother and me. So in my mind, that meant I was fully qualified to know how to raise Codey and Casey. A blended family is hard enough but having a stubborn husband with no experience raising kids that thinks he knows it all doesn't help. With my controlling ways, I seemed to completely forget what the counselor had advised.

The arguments between Donna and me came when the boys messed up. Whether it was their behavior or their grades, I always harped on what the punishment should be. I thought Donna wasn't strict enough. If one of the boys got a C in a class, I wanted to put them in technology prison—no TV or video games for a month.

Actions have consequences, but I learned over the years if discipline doesn't come out of love, it won't change behavior. My focus should have been—like Donna's—on helping them improve. Instead, I tended to berate them for the mistake rather than talking through what happened and helping them see how they could handle the situation differently the next time. Fortunately, Codey and Casey have turned into great men, and we are very proud of them.

Another regret with the boys was not eating and praying together, which was completely my fault. After we'd been living together just a few weeks they asked me if they could eat dinner in their room while playing video games. I thought that was a great idea since it meant some quiet time with Donna. Of course, that became the habit. Big mistake. Once again, I made a rationalization based on selfishness.

I am sorry for all the opportunities we lost to have family time around the dinner table. We could have encouraged the boys to talk about their day and be more a part of each other's lives. Family dinners are also a great way to take turns leading prayer. Like too many people, for a long time I was uncomfortable praying in front of others. When I was a child, in my family it was always my dad who prayed, and I had no practice. Somehow, I had the idea that I had to pray certain words. My prayer life changed dramatically when I realized God doesn't care about my words, He cares about my heart. In recent years, I have come to believe my "best" prayers have been the ones I don't even recall what I said because I let Holy Spirit speak through me. These are lessons I wish we would have taught our sons at an earlier age.

I mentioned that I also had a bad temper back then. What do I mean? In 2007 I was watching a football game between the University of Louisville and the University of Connecticut. The refs completely missed a fair catch call and UConn ran it back for a touchdown. I was so angry I jumped up and left the room. Cussing the refs and walking down the hallway, I put my fist through the wall. Staring at the hole, I immediately knew I'd blown it. Clips of that call are still on YouTube and I think the caption calling it one of the worst calls in football history is fair. That still doesn't justify putting a hole in the wall. Nothing justified doing that. I'm sure you can guess the impact my thoughtless action had on our boys.

I also continued to drink, and I am embarrassed to say I even drank with our boys during their later high school and college years. I matured slowly, but I can trace the beginning of a change to when we started getting involved at a new church.

Donna's Testimony

I was amazed that John was willing to step up and accept the responsibility of an instant family. That was huge! He had no idea what he was getting into, nor did I. . . .

Once we were engaged, when John wanted to consolidate everything and move in together, I knew it wasn't right, but I didn't say anything. Contrary to what John and I told each other, I told the boys we were only doing it because we were getting married. Not just for convenience. I didn't want to rock the boat, and John was adamant about it. I wasn't strong enough at the time to stand up for what was right.

I immediately discovered *how much* of a list-maker John is. He wrote lists for everything! Yes, I made fun of all his lists, but they did mean John took care of *all* the planning and details for the wedding. I stayed with friends the night before and only had to show up. How cool is that!

I think we picked the hottest day of the year. We had a Jamaican theme and got married by our pool. Our boys were the only two that stood up front with us, other than John's dad who married us. Everyone dressed in casual attire and brought swimwear for afterward. And, yes, our family and friends were quite familiar with John and his lists, which made the "List Burning Ceremony" that much better.

Now it was time for us, as husband and wife, to parent our boys.

Once John told Casey and Codey they could eat in their rooms, things went south. Like John said, we didn't eat together—but *none* of us even ate at the table. John would fill the dining room table with a smorgasbord of junk food, chips, pop tarts, cans of Mountain Dew, Big Red, and A & W root beer and top it off with stuff like Little Debbie's Swiss Rolls. For "meat," he liked pizza rolls from the freezer. I basically lived at a college frat house. John and I ate in front of the TV while the boys played their video games. I thought John, as the father figure, should set a good example. I was expecting him to lead instead of being one of them. But instead of speaking up, I contributed to the problem by not saying anything.

When the boys witnessed John put his hand through the wall, that gave them instant permission to react the same way. Sure enough, a couple of times, Casey punched a hole in his wall when he got mad playing video games. If you're wondering how we disciplined him for that, here's what happened. He hid the holes by rearranging his furniture and we never even discovered them until we moved. By then Casey was out of the house and living on his own.

Remember that agreement we'd made in counseling that I would be the one to enforce discipline? As soon as the boys messed up, John was in my face. "What are you going to do? What did you say?" I felt like he was glad they were getting in trouble! As far as their grades, if they were working hard, I was happy. Casey is an active learner. The school wanted him on medication for ADHD, but I didn't want to drug him. Active learners learn through movement, so school is often harder for them. We got Casey a tutor for a while, and I worked with him every night on schoolwork. If he still got a C in a class, I was okay with it.

At times John accused me of paying more attention to the boys than to him. We started scheduling date nights and alone time when I realized he was right. Besides helping Casey with homework, during those years I was also supporting Codey through additional surgeries. Along with the cleft lip and palate he'd had surgery for when he was a baby, his gum overlapped on the cleft side. He had no bone in that area and no tooth had developed.

At age nine he had to get braces to widen that area and prepare for a bone graft, which would come from his hip. Codey had the surgery when he was ten years old. My heart hurt for him: he went in the hospital feeling completely fine and woke up in pain and unable to walk. The spot where they removed bone from his hip hurt worse than all the work in his mouth. Plus . . . he was disappointed that now, with that area closed in, he couldn't squirt milk out of his nose anymore. Who knew? I told him he would thank me someday.

The doctors said he would walk again in about a week after coming out of the hospital, but Codey had other plans. Just days after Codey's surgery, the movie *Ice Age* was coming out and his goal was to walk in to see it. Also, that same weekend his grandma was coming to visit. Codey worked so hard on his own—first crawling, then making himself walk, using furniture or anything he could find to help hold him up while he tried. Opening night of the film, just two days after leaving the hospital, Codey gave all he had to walk up to the door of the theater. What determination in such a young man. He was so proud when his grandma arrived, and he could walk to her!

Two years later, when Codey was twelve, he had surgery on his nose. When he was little his nose had looked normal, but as he grew it was obvious it wasn't developing correctly—it was flat and kind of leaning to the left, and it was making it harder for him to breathe through it. His doctor tried to repair and reshape it. Codey went through a lot of pain, but after that surgery, he still had difficulty breathing through his nose, and his nose still was misshapen.

Fortunately, we were eventually told about a surgeon who could actually rebuild Codey's nose, but Codey had to be eighteen years old. It turned out that Codey's nose had no cartilage, so the doctor took cartilage from his ear to rebuild it. I hated that he had to wait that long, but this surgeon did an amazing job! We will be forever grateful for him and how God led us to him through a recommendation from a friend.

I was truly blessed with our boys. I believe that was a result of prayer. And I prayed A LOT! I was afraid that as they got into their teen years, they would become disrespectful and try my authority, and John's authority when he came on board. But by the grace of God, when they disagreed with us, they were still respectful. They never talked back to us. They respected John, and I don't think they ever felt like he shouldn't be there. We kept them in the Catholic school system through twelfth grade. We could have bought a small island for the price of tuition for two boys, but I believe it was worth it. It was also nice going to church as a family. As they got older, they did ask me what their options were about going to church—and I told them Saturday afternoon, or two choices on Sunday: the early or the late service! I had vowed to take them to church, and

I did. Even when they had friends over on Saturday night, it was understood that we all would be going to church on Sunday.

My biggest struggle was with John's drinking. When I was a little girl, I didn't have a choice and had to be around the chaos alcoholics make, but I wasn't going to now. I would have a drink occasionally, but it wasn't a temptation for me; I knew the ugly side of it. John, on the other hand, thought it wasn't worth going someplace if alcohol was not available. Thank God he didn't get mean when he drank, but he still drank to excess. He could be okay one minute and toast the next, falling down, slurring his words. By then, it was too late for me to convince him to cut himself off. More than once, I had to stop John from peeing in the closet. Fun times.

In addition, something new arrived during our early years of marriage. I'm just going to say it . . . menopause! It hit me hard. I had three older sisters and not one warned me. I had no idea what was going on, but I could pull your heart right out of your chest, and I may or may not feel bad about it. It's a miracle John stayed! The tables turned, and I was the one in *his* face.

As a side note, have you tried to teach two teenage boys to drive while going through that!? Casey waited to learn to drive a year longer than he needed to after he saw what Codey went through to get his license. God bless those boys! I'm confident they can handle anything that comes at them while driving a car, thanks to me. You're welcome.

So, like any marriage, ours had its challenges. But John and I were committed to making our marriage work, and divorce was not an option. I knew my attitude was up to me regardless of what he did or said. When the challenges came, I knew my old self would have run; but instead of running, I decided to give the situation to God. What an idea! I told God everything I was feeling, and I realized the only person I had control of was me. I asked God to help me with my issues and started praying *for* John (which I had not done in previous relationships). I let go of my desire to change him and let God deal with both of us. That's when our relationship started to change.

Self-Reflection

Rationalization can be described as "a defense mechanism when controversial behaviors or feelings are justified and explained in a seemingly rational or logical manner (to avoid) the true reason for the behavior."[1]

Maybe you have heard someone say that everyone has their own truth. That statement couldn't be more wrong. There is one Truth, and we can find it in the Word of God. In his gospel, John wrote, "Jesus said to the people who believed in Him, 'You are truly my disciples if you remain faithful to my teachings. And you will know the truth, and the truth will set you free'" (John 8:31-32).

John's dad gave us powerful advice for marriage when he said, "A big key to success in marriage is to put God first, then husband and wife, and then the kids." (But most people get this completely backward, putting the kids first, then the marriage relationship, and turning to God last.) It took us time to learn to apply this, but as we did, we learned that the more we put God first, going to Him with our questions, needs and issues, the more everything fell into place.

For example, one way to help stay focused on the truth is to have an accountability partner, someone you can talk to about potential decisions . . . and just as important, someone that will recognize when you are headed down a bad path and will redirect you. God can help connect you with wise accountability partners—just like He did with us. So, although we didn't start out in our relationship following this advice, we do today, and now we receive invaluable advice from others. John has a few men that fill these roles—including a trusted friend, and an ex-boss who helps him with work decisions. And Donna's transparency in her ladies' small groups opens the door for encouragement and direction.

- Has there been something in your life you have rationalized, even though it is contrary to God's Word? What price did you pay? Are you rationalizing anything now? About what? What will you do about it?

- It can be easy to rationalize a decision based on what we want. Do you have an unbiased accountability partner you can discuss potential decisions with? If you go to God, He will help connect you with one.

- As you look back on your mistakes, what can you learn from them and apply today?

---

[1] Nurse Plus Academy - https://nurse.plus/nclex-terminology/terms-abbreviations/rationalization/

The human body has many parts, but the many parts make up one whole body. So it is with the body of Christ. Some of us are Jews, some are Gentiles, some are slaves, and some are free. But we have all been baptized into one body by one Spirit, and we all share in the same Spirit.

—I Corinthians 12:12-13

Chapter 6

SPIRITUAL AWAKENING

John's Testimony

A s the priest spoke, all I could think about was the gossip going around about him. Was it true that he didn't respect women? Could it be true that he laundered money from his last parish? Did he really hate kids? On our way home, as Donna and I talked, we discovered we both felt we were missing something. We realized we were focusing on the problems at the church rather than listening for what God was trying to tell us during the services.

It was fall 2011. Both Casey and Codey had graduated from high school and were living on their own. In the six years Donna and I had been married, we had both gotten very active in the church. We sang in the choir, volunteered at events, and I even served on the parish council, a leadership team that advises the priest. We had a lot of friends there and a core group with whom we'd often share meals. But even those good friendships didn't make up for what we were missing during services. Maybe it was time to try somewhere else.

We were already involved at the non-denominational Christian church my boss attended. Shortly after Donna and I had started dating, I left our joint employer and took a position at a lumber company. My boss, Steve, quickly became more than just a boss. He became, and still is, my mentor, a close friend, and accountability partner. He certainly has helped me in my career, but more importantly, he helped me become a better man, husband, and stepfather. Steve lives Proverbs 27:17: "As iron sharpens iron, so a friend sharpens a friend."

After I'd worked with Steve a couple of years, he invited me to his men's group at his church. I discovered the power of strong men sharing their hearts, goals, struggles, and victories. Challenging each other. Praying for each other. We became brothers. I also helped Steve organize the kids' basketball league and went on a few golf trips with the church. Donna and Steve's wife, Dee Dee, became friends and they were in a small group together as well.

Although we had been involved at Steve's church for several years, we'd never been to a service. But now, with everything going on at our church, Donna and I decided to give it a try. I told Steve we'd see him Sunday.

"Uhh . . . this might not be the best weekend to come," he responded. Steve knew my ideas about baptism and that Sunday they were starting a series called "Immersion." He knew I wouldn't agree with how baptism would be presented and was afraid it would scare me off. I was curious and a bit challenged by his words—and I was determined to give their service a shot. That decision would change the course of my faith journey.

Our first impressions were mixed. As we walked into the church several different people enthusiastically greeted us, making us feel welcome. The music was uplifting and joyful—though a little too loud. And I wasn't too sure about clapping during church. There were even a couple of people raising their hands in worship. That was certainly weird for me. Up to then, I'd considered anything over a ten-minute sermon too long, but the preacher talked almost half the service. However, I was so engaged that I didn't notice it was that long. The message referenced numerous Bible verses and I was taking notes. I didn't agree with some of the points, but the preacher's words inspired me to do some research. I read my Bible more the week following that service than I had the entire previous five years. Steve was right; I disagreed with the church's theology of baptism. It didn't scare me off, but my struggle with that lasted for several years.

Despite a few theological differences, we officially joined that church soon after. As our church home, it helped me strengthen my relationship with the Father, Son, and Holy Spirit, and it stretched me outside my comfort zone. At that time, I would have preferred to walk in, talk only to those I knew, and take my seat. But Donna and I became door greeters, so each week I found myself being what I would call overly friendly to a bunch of people I didn't know. I loved it.

Our circle of friends expanded, and we were filled spiritually each time we attended; Donna and I felt God was speaking directly to each of us with the message. When we ended up moving to Florida, we didn't think we would be able to find a church home like it. However, God's plans are always greater than our own.

Within Christian churches, different denominations have different strengths and appeals. In my experience, the Catholic church provides beautiful ceremonies, and long-held traditions followed in a more formal, subdued service. My sense of the Lutheran churches I attended was similar—they had a more formal service. One strength of non-denominational churches, with their more informal service, is a focus on relationship: personal relationship with fellow church members, and personal relationship with Jesus and Holy Spirit.

I am thankful for the foundation I received from both the Lutheran and the Catholic church. However, my faith journey intensified when I chose growth and started focusing on my relationship with Jesus and with Holy Spirit who lives inside me.

For example, at the time, I didn't realize Holy Spirit was speaking to me when we decided to try a new church. I would have called it a gut decision or just something I sensed God was directing me to do. After years of prayer and growth, I can now look back with confidence that Holy Spirit was speaking directly to me. He was convicting, not condemning, me about thoughts I was having about the priest. Whether those thoughts were justified or not, they were used to change my path and I am eternally grateful. When faced with decisions today, I ask Holy Spirit for guidance and confirmation. I ask for closed doors just as much as open ones. Answers don't always come in the timing I'd like, but I know when I experience peace with the decision, Holy Spirit has settled my soul and I can proceed with boldness and confidence.

Donna's Testimony

"And then, the heavenly Father said, 'Come into the light, baby girl, and dance with me.'" As I watched the video in our small group, tears streamed down my face. I was His baby girl!

I had been drawn into Dee Dee's ladies' group by its title, "When Wallflowers Dance." We were reading Angela Thomas' book of the same name and each week we enjoyed her video lesson. I could relate to being a wallflower, against the wall, invisible, and basically stuck in a dark corner, chained to the baggage I was carrying. In her book, Angela reveals her struggles, including finding herself a single mom with small children to raise. She talked about God as a loving father that wanted His baby girl to come into the light and dance with Him!

Growing up Baptist, I was used to services on Sunday morning, Sunday night, and Wednesday night. There were Sunday school classes for all ages. We had Bible drills and memorized Bible verses. We had an adult choir, children's choir, and more: youth retreats, choir performances at other churches, church-wide celebrations, and tent revivals. I always participated in the choir, where we enjoyed our congregation's energetic support: if people were moved by a song, they clapped. And even when we messed up a song, there was always at least one enthusiastic "Amen!" And, of course, where two or more were gathered, there was a casserole.

We started attending the Catholic church because Casey and Codey were in school there. It didn't make sense to continue going back and forth to my Baptist church three times a week while the boys were developing friendships at school, and I was getting to know the parents. The Catholic church was completely different from what I was used to. Like John, I felt it was more restrained. When the choir finished a moving song, you could hear crickets. Every now and then, when the priest would mention the choir before he began the homily, there would be some polite applause. I understood—it was just different. We went to church on Sunday for about forty-five minutes and that was basically it for the week unless we count bingo.

In February 2004, when John and I had been dating for about three months, the boys and I moved down the street from the Catholic church. The location was perfect for us. I was close to work and, once they were a little older, the boys could walk home from school. I was blessed with a flexible work schedule, so I could take them to school, go to work and pick them up in the afternoon. I appreciated that when the boys started driving, they could return the favor, dropping me off at work, driving to school and then picking *me* up.

When John started going to the men's' group and helping at Steve's church, I saw that he was meeting a lot of people. Meanwhile, I missed being involved in studies and church activities and making friends at church. When Steve's wife, Dee Dee, invited me to join her study, I overcame my discomfort about driving seventeen miles alone at night to a church where I knew only one person—and said yes. That Bible study started my spiritual awakening.

I found the study so powerful that I took that ladies' Bible study to our Catholic church. It was different from anything our church had been doing, but I think it was a welcomed change. When I introduced the study, I joked, "I grew up Baptist and we did Bible drills, but then I joined the Catholic church, and I haven't seen a Bible since"—and the ladies laughed!

When John suggested going to an actual service at the non-denominational church, I was interested in trying it out, but I knew I wouldn't be as comfortable since I didn't know many people there like he did. That church was also bigger than churches I was used to attending. And the worship: no hymnal . . . no choir. . . . What??? The music was contemporary, with the words on the screen. I didn't know the songs, so I was a little taken aback. That all changed when the pastor spoke. I was moved more in that one sermon than I had been in ten years. John said it perfectly: I felt God was speaking to me through the pastor's words. My fear of going to a new church was instantly gone. I was captivated. I was home.

Self-Reflection

There is a specific local church for each of us in different seasons of our spiritual journey that will help us grow our relationship with each person of the Trinity: Father (God), Son (Jesus), and Holy Spirit. If you feel you may not be in the church that will best help you grow, consider visiting other churches. When we moved to Florida, it was important to us that we find a church that offered small groups and outreach programs, where we'd have the opportunity to serve in the community.

We suggest checking out a helpful article, "Looking for the 'Right' Church?" by Robert Velarde, published in 2008 at FocusOnTheFamly.com.[2]

When we visit a church, sometimes we focus on what we don't like about the structure of a service, and our attitude can hinder us from hearing from Holy Spirit *through* the service. Rather than focusing on what we don't like, let's pray that our eyes, ears, and heart will be open, and we will receive what God wants to deliver regardless of how it's presented.

How do you know when Holy Spirit is talking to you? His voice is that small inner voice you hear. Some often call it a gut feeling. Some call it their conscience. As you see in our story, for years we said it was God speaking to us. Talking about Holy Spirit brings up questions: Does Holy Spirit only talk to believers? How do I know it's Holy Spirit rather than my own fears or desires? A terrific book for this topic is *The God I Never Knew* by Robert Morris.

In the Old Testament, there were laws to follow to come into God's presence. Holy Spirit's anointing would descend and then leave. But everything changed with Jesus. Through the sacrifice of His death and resurrection, He restored the relationship between us sinful, fallen beings and God. He gives us Holy Spirit, a gift that can live in each of us. Our lives will change forever when we realize the power that lives in us. Holy Spirit is our friend. He doesn't want to be kept in a backpack and only brought out when things go bad or at dinner when we give thanks. He wants to be involved in every detail of our lives. God does not want the rules of religion to be our focus. Our focus should always be on God and having a personal relationship with Him. A good local church is the best place to help develop that.

---

[2] Find it at https://www.focusonthefamily.com/faith/looking-for-the-right-church/

- Have you found a local church you are happy to call home? If not, what steps can you take to find one?

- What is your relationship with Holy Spirit? Does the church you attend help you develop a closer relationship with Him?

- Are you in a small group? If not, will you commit to joining one? When?

Work willingly at whatever you do, as though you were working for the Lord rather than for people. Remember that the Lord will give you an inheritance as your reward, and that the Master you are serving is Christ.

—Colossians 3:23-24

Chapter 7

WORKING
FOR THE LORD

John's Testimony

"**A**re you going to be a pastor?"

I've lost count of the number of times I heard that question growing up. My dad and grandfather were both pastors, so people assumed I would follow in their footsteps. I always laughed it off and said no because I had big plans in the business world. But inside I was saying no because I didn't think I was good enough. I wasn't exactly modeling my life in the way Jesus did. Then, many years later, I started to feel guilty about business successes I was seeing. I wondered if I should exit the business world to work in ministry.

Look at what Satan was doing. When I was a young man, he was telling me I wasn't good enough to lead others to God. After some success in the business world, he was putting guilt in my mind that I wasn't following God's plan for my life and was chasing success and money. There were some partial truths on both counts, but Satan was using those to keep me from living the life God desired. Although I was a Christian, for many of my choices, I didn't think about God's purpose and plan for my life. That was especially true when I was a kid.

I'm embarrassed to remember my selfish attitude toward my first job, delivering papers with my dad. He helped me put the papers together and drove the car, covering all the transportation costs, and giving all his time. I carried the papers to the doorsteps. We split the pay fifty-fifty. I let him know I didn't think that was fair. He pointed out, "I have to pay for gas. This route is miles away from our house. If it wasn't for me, you couldn't even have the job." Back then, I was still resentful. Now, of course, I'm just grateful for the opportunity I had to earn some money and have time alone with my father.

My dad also taught me that verse from Colossians about working as for the Lord. It took me time, but as I worked and grew in my relationship with God, He began to guide me to fulfill my purpose.

I first had an inkling about God having plans for me at age fifteen. That was when my dad felt called to be the sole pastor at a church in Louisville, and we made that move that I was so against at the time. Once I got there, I quickly recognized God had plans for me as well. An elder at the church, Wayne, let our family live with him and his wife for several weeks while my parents looked for a home. Wayne, a top salesperson at a refrigeration company, got me a job there and became my first mentor. I took note of why he did so well: he was a hard worker, had great people skills, and made the customers feel like he was there to help them, not just close a deal.

I started out cleaning used equipment, getting it ready for resale. I was able to go in after school and work a few hours each day and full-time in the summer. I was thrilled to have a job and got satisfaction from seeing the quick transformation from a dirty piece of equipment to something ready to be resold.

By the end of summer, I was moved to the walk-in cooler manufacturing department. It was a small area with only three other guys. Once I learned the fabrication process, they allowed me to work late and get extra hours after they left. Their trust made me want to pour even more into the job. I was given responsibility and I took pride in my work.

Shortly after I started college at the University of Louisville in 1997, the company moved me to the office. I learned AutoCAD, a drafting software we used to draw architectural plans for customers, and then was given some sales responsibilities, mostly handling the call-in customers. With Wayne guiding me, I started seeing some success. I was blessed with a great model in Wayne. He taught me if I would use the Golden Rule with customers, "Do to others whatever you would like them to do to you" (Matt 7:12), I would see business success.

I started out with a major in accounting but in my junior year, I changed it to marketing, thinking that would help me more in a sales career. Over the next few years, I learned a lot, but I wasn't completely happy. I found out that I didn't like the sales side of things. I told myself that I wasn't a people-person. Regardless of my successes, I dwelled on the sales I didn't get. I was searching, but I wasn't going to God for answers. And while I did recognize the path God had set in front of me with Wayne and the opportunity I was given at the company, I wanted more. More responsibility. More money. And of course, I wanted everything NOW.

I worked for and with a great group of people. They gave me the flexibility to go to school and take off when needed. However, I didn't think I had much room to advance there: the vice president was young, and the owner had two sons, both about to graduate from college, who might get involved. I looked for another company, but I didn't burn any bridges; I worked on AutoCAD drawings on the side for them for several years after I left.

The job interview couldn't have gone better. "Well, John, your resume is impressive, and I like your attitude," the hiring manager told me. "I think you'll be a real asset to this company. We'd like you to start as soon as possible." I didn't know anything about air conditioning, but the job sounded like a great opportunity. They hired me as a "Management Trainee." Right from the beginning, they would have their sights on me becoming management, right? Surely this was God opening a door!

I would love to say that I took time to pray, ask for God's wisdom, and seek wise counsel, but I was so excited to receive a job offer right on the spot that I said yes immediately.

That "great opportunity" ended up being a bust. The job was 100 percent sales, and it was purely cold calling. I was landing some new business, including a large project at Louisville's Baptist seminary, but sales mean a lot of rejections, and I'm not wired to just let those roll off my back. It didn't matter that I had some success. I couldn't get past all the no's. The lie I was believing, that I wasn't a people-person, continued to build. In my mind, the rejections were proof of that.

This experience was a good example of how God protected me even when I wasn't seeking Him. After less than a year, in 2001, I went to work for an ice machine distributor. Shortly after I left the air conditioning company, the manager was caught stealing and several people went down with him. I never witnessed anything, but I'm grateful God removed me from the situation.

Working at the ice machine distributor seemed perfect. I knew the owner and most of their workers already. Back when I was at the refrigeration company, I was successful selling ice machines that we purchased from this distributor. They would frequently send me leads since I landed a good percentage of them. This was also the company where I met Donna, so there is no doubt God had a plan there.

Once again, I was working for a great person and with a great group of people. My new boss, Rod, was a good Christian man who is married to Donna's sister Carol. I can still remember the first family Christmas gathering I went to with Donna. Just before opening presents, Rod gathered the kids around, opened his clearly well-read Bible, and read them the Christmas story. Rod didn't shy away from talking about Jesus at the workplace either. His whole extended family treated him with respect.

Right after I was hired, a friend from high school asked if I was interested in coming to his work as a truss designer at a lumber company. I explained that I had just changed jobs and wasn't looking. God's timing and protection had my back yet again. A few years later, the truss designers hired around this time were the ones laid off during the housing crisis of 2008.

I worked for the ice machine distributor for about two years and attended graduate school at night. I loved many aspects of my new position. Rod involved me in purchasing decisions and I discovered I loved analyzing the forecasts and sales trends and determining what inventory we should be stocking. I loved taking orders and helping customers get what they needed. Two of the other workers taught me about the parts we sold and the inner workings of an ice machine. I couldn't have asked for a better training environment and team setting.

However, part of my job was cold calling. We handled a few deliveries and while out, I was asked to stop by places that we weren't currently selling to. Rejections over the phone were hard enough, but I was getting rejected by the receptionists at front desks and not getting to talk to decision-makers. Though this was only a small portion of the job, I hated it and chose to focus on that. I let that affect my entire attitude. On days I didn't have any sales calls scheduled, I would arrive early with excitement to tackle the tasks of the day.

On sales call days I told myself in advance that I would be seeing rejection, and I struggled to roll out of bed.

As usual, I worked hard, did the best I could, and worked extra hours. They kept track of comp time and my hours piled up. One day I had a particularly difficult college exam and asked Rod if I could leave at lunch to take the afternoon to prepare. He asked, "Do you have any comp time?" Looking back, I see he didn't mean anything by the question, but at the time, I took it personally.

"How could he have not recognized all the extra hours I had been working? Why would he even have to ask that?" I fumed. I felt like I had been slapped in the face. I viewed Rod's question as rejection from someone I respected. By this time Donna and I were dating, and I felt it would be better that we not work at the same company. All this on top of my growing discomfort with sales caused me soon after to start looking for another job.

In February 2004, I went to work at that lumber company where my friend had asked me to take a truss designer job. But now I was hired as an engineered wood products (EWP) designer. There I met Steve, who would become my mentor and close friend. I used engineering software to design floor systems and calculate supporting beams. The experience from using AutoCAD years earlier at the refrigeration company came in handy. I loved it. God doesn't waste any of our skills.

I felt a part of the team right from the start. The sales staff made me feel needed and constantly thanked me for my work. After having worked in sales, I knew I had the opportunity to make their job easier. More than just providing the designs, I created the quotes for them and kept them updated on when to expect this information back. It's amazing how much good communication can improve a process.

My immediate boss, Jerry, taught me everything he knew about EWP and the lumber business. He was a deacon at a local Catholic church, and we had some lively conversations about faith as well. It wouldn't be unusual to hear Steve, Jerry, and me discussing a hot topic like the theology of baptism while on break. These types of topics used to energize me, and I enjoyed the debates. However, I have come to realize these can quickly turn into arguments that Satan uses as weapons to divide Christians. When my passion for what in my mind was the "right" way turned into putting other denominations down, I was focusing on religion and not how we all should have relationship with Jesus and each other.

My bosses taught me to respond to the needs of the company's employees. Steve and Jerry would frequently counsel employees. I remember one day they talked to one of our workers whose wife had just left him. They set work aside and comforted him the best they could.

I can't thank Jerry enough for allowing me to work on other projects even though they weren't in his department. Steve was Jerry's boss, so Steve could ask me to do anything he wanted, but Jerry could have kept me down and held a grudge. Instead, Jerry encouraged me to learn as much as I could from Steve and said it wouldn't surprise him if I didn't last long in his department. Jerry was a God-centered leader. He put what was best for me above what was best for him. If I left, he would have to start all over with someone new, but that didn't matter to him. He had pride watching me grow in the company. That was a guy who was working as for the Lord.

Steve was another one like Jerry. He took me under his wing. I was blessed again that those in leadership poured into me. I sat right outside his office and 99 percent of the time his door was open. I heard conversations with everyone from the high school kids sweeping floors to the owner of the company. He started from the ground floor in the company as an inside sales rep and had reached a vice president position. He remembered his roots and talked to everyone with the same friendly tone. It's amazing how much I learned just by listening.

Steve quickly assigned additional responsibilities to me such as purchasing and operations. I even sat in on some job interviews. Steve's leadership ability drew me in. His approach was to involve in the decision-making process the people that would be affected by the final decision. He tried to let them put together the plan and would only come in and mandate things when necessary. He listened before he talked. He wasn't a hand wringer though. He would gather people, discuss, make a team decision, and move on. Rehashing decisions? Inefficient.

Shortly before the 2008 housing crisis, the company decided to change their point-of-sale software. Steve attended the first meeting, but after that, he told me to go in his place. By then I understood the sales, purchasing, and operations side of our existing software, and he felt I'd be more valuable than he would be learning the new software early. I was honored, and each time he elevated me, I was determined to perform up to his faith in me.

I enjoyed being part of the process and at twenty-nine was the youngest in the core group. As we were getting close to conversion time, our information technology manager in charge of the project was behind in training the employees. The company moved me from my position to focus solely on the conversion. I learned everyone's job functions and developed customized training documentation including screenshots from the new software to help them transition from the old system to the new. I led the training classes and after conversion, I was on the phone non-stop for a couple of months helping people. I didn't recognize it at the time, but the satisfaction I received from helping others helped me begin to realize I was, in fact, a people-person. This was when I first started having clarity about my purpose in the business world.

I knew the IT manager was going to retire once things settled down after the conversion, but I never dreamed that would affect me. He managed two people, and it turned out that close to 75 percent of his job was financial reporting. One day Steve asked me, "What do you think about becoming the IT manager?" He knew I would excel at the financial reporting side and thought I was ready to take the step into management.

I said, "Just because I know more about technology than the average lumber yard guy, doesn't mean I know networks and hardware."

Steve explained, "The others in the department understand that part. We need someone to manage the department that will prioritize based on what Operations needs, and you understand our operations. I think you would be a great fit and I am recommending you for the position." His confidence in me was all I needed to accept the new role.

It was nice that the transition was over three months. I was able to learn information management programs like Crystal Reports, Microsoft Access, and a little bit of SQL, or Structured Query Language, used for database management systems. When the old IT manager retired, I knew what I needed to keep the financial reporting side going. However, I still knew nothing about the IT side.

Suddenly, three months into my new position, both guys working in IT left the same week. While they never told me this directly, I think they resented not getting the job. Though I could see their point (I was younger, newer, and didn't know IT), I took it personally when they left shortly after I started.

Instead of hiring replacements, we decided to interview an outside company. The night before that meeting our email and document server were both deleted. We never did prove who it was, but I can tell you those were some of the most stressful days in my career. I oversaw a department that now had no actual people in it and had no clue how to fix anything. We hired the outside company instantly because we were desperate. I screamed out loud at night, "Where are you, God? Why would you give me this great opportunity and then leave me?" I was ready to quit because I had no answers.

After what seemed like weeks but was only a few days, the outside company was able to recover 75 percent of what had been deleted. The backups hadn't run as frequently as they should have—maybe a mistake on the part of the guy (not me!) who set them up. After a couple of months, things calmed down.

But the calm wouldn't last long. In a short period of time, the owner of the company passed away and the housing crisis hit. Layoffs had started, though I felt safe given no one else knew how to do what I was doing. This was another example of God putting me in places. Had I still been in the EWP department, I would have likely been let go.

The company controller, Eric, announced he was taking a position at a large health insurance company. It was a great opportunity for him, and he made the transition with integrity. He gave three weeks' notice and offered to come back at night if needed to help train his successor. I respected Eric and had worked closely with him since he was the main person to whom I sent the financial reports.

I had always liked accounting and by this point had obtained my MBA. Given the state of the economy, I was sure we could manage things without hiring someone. I could take some of Eric's responsibilities and portion out the rest. Plus, I hated IT. I couldn't care less about fixing a printer or network problems and still didn't have expertise in that area. I made my case to the president and Steve. Steve didn't say much, but I found out the president decided to hold interviews with people outside the company.

I was livid. I had made a strong case. They weren't going to find a person outside the company that cared as much as I did. My work ethic was never questioned. I said this and much worse in an email to the president. Not only did I not seek God's guidance, I didn't let anyone else read the email before I clicked send. Quite frankly, I could have been fired for some of the things I said. I questioned the president's leadership and his decision-making. Pride settled in thick, and my email had no filter. Thankfully Steve stepped in and made peace. The three of us had a conversation—in person—and ultimately, they did decide to shift responsibilities and not hire anyone. God, and the company president, showed me grace big time.

The transition went well, and Eric was true to his word. Well past a month after he left, he came back to help with the bank reconciliation and a few other items. We also hired someone else to work in the IT department. He technically worked for me, but between him and the outside contractor, I rarely had to get involved. I loved the new position. There was a great team in accounting working with me. They came to work every day and didn't need me micromanaging them. I used the leadership skills I had learned from Wayne, Rod, and Steve, and felt good about where my career was going. Everyone felt we were a team, and I was there to help them.

However, yet again, soon that wasn't enough. I always saw myself following in Steve's footsteps. I thought there was more prestige in managing the company's largest location over being the controller. About a year later, it turned out that Eric wasn't happy in the big corporate world and was talking about returning. Steve wanted me to come out and run the lumber yard since he was taking on more responsibilities for the company as a whole and needed someone to run operations at the location. Eric's returning would make for an easy transition. My dream job was coming true!

Donna's Testimony

As I look back over my career life, I am amazed at how God has protected me, blessed me again and again, and even moved me around—ultimately to the company where I met John, my soulmate and partner.

When I was in high school, to me and those around me, it seemed that the acceptable jobs for women were nurses, teachers, or secretaries. I knew I didn't have what it took to be a nurse. I was afraid of people and certainly didn't want to be responsible for causing them pain. Teaching was completely out of the question—even teaching Sunday school and Vacation Bible School, I still reacted to kids like I was being attacked. So on to business classes I went.

After I graduated from high school, my sister Carol told me about the need for key-punch operators now that computers were becoming popular. Yep, I go that far back. I didn't even know what a key-punch operator was, so I took a four-week class and was hired by a tabulating company in downtown Louisville. They specialized in generating key-punch work for small companies. For those that have no idea what I'm talking about, the keypunch machine was a glorified keyboard. I would type information normally, and the machine would transform the information into computer language by punching holes into cards at specific locations. The cards would then be fed into a computer that would read the information. (I'm talking about one computer large enough to be maintained in a temperature-controlled room of its own.) I was eighteen years old.

A couple of God stories happened during the two years I worked at the tabulating company. A new section of I-264 West, the route I took to work, had just opened and connected to I-64 going downtown. This improvement was a big deal for Louisville. The new extension followed the Ohio River and was raised above the city to prevent flooding. There was even a heated exit ramp installed at 9th Street that eliminated ice forming on this steep ramp.

During this time my dad was riding with a coworker, so I could take his car. Some days this was a real challenge, since Dad was never big on maintaining his cars. I often needed to put water in the radiator to get to work, again to go home, and again if I was going somewhere after work. The car leaked oil, so I added that regularly too. I was very familiar with driving a car with no heat in Louisville winters where the average low in January is 25 degrees. "Just put some coolant on the windows, inside and out, to keep your windows from freezing," Dad nonchalantly advised me.

I made sure I stayed in the correct lane all the way to work so I wouldn't have to change lanes; I knew I wouldn't have been able to see. That worked great until I got off that heated ramp. A car was stalled on the ramp, and I could not see to get around. Cars were coming off at 55 miles an hour! I was crying out to God and scraping the windows on the *inside* so I could see. Out of nowhere, a man came up and asked if I was okay. He said, "You don't have heat in that car!?" That man stood out there in the freezing cold and stopped the traffic coming down that ramp so I could get around the stalled car. I know God sent him to rescue me.

The second time still sends chills when I think about it. Again, I was going to work down I-264. The semi-truck right in front of me suddenly hit his brakes. Luckily, there was an extra lane forming on my right to allow for traffic coming on the expressway from the street. I had to swerve into that lane to get out of his way. My first reaction was to continue ahead of him, but I heard that familiar voice tell me not to. So instead, I slowly pulled up beside him . . . and I saw a little girl in her pajamas, a stuffed animal in her left hand, walking in front of his truck. She ran her right hand across the grill of his truck, then grinned as she walked past my car. She climbed over the guardrail and down the hill she went. Neither of us could move until she was out of sight.

After these two events, you might think I would be able to trust God. But, nope, I forgot all about them. It was only much later, as my relationship with Him grew, that Holy Spirit reminded me of these situations. I'm so grateful and thankful for His protection, even though I didn't recognize it at the time.

At the tabulating company, a coworker and I became friends and decided to get an apartment together. I loved her family and hung out with them regularly. Her aunt was a key-punch operator for a distillery. When another key-punch operator position became available, she asked me to apply for it and I was hired. I didn't drink, and from time to time, given my family history, I felt convicted about working at a place that made and sold alcohol. But I didn't act on my convictions. I'm ashamed to say I just took the job and stayed there. It was convenient. It paid benefits.

One benefit was education. The company offered paid tuition programs, so I worked days and went to school in the evenings. I was twenty when I started there. I chose to go to community college first for general courses and planned to apply to Bellarmine College (now University) for my degree. While I attended community college I moved back home, saved the money to buy a house, and got married the first time. As I mentioned in an earlier chapter, I had just gotten accepted to Bellarmine when, after six years with the distillery, I was let go, one month after my dad died. Although I didn't have the courage to leave a company in an industry I felt uncomfortable working in, God made the move for me.

At the time, my brother-in-law, Rod, was the only employee at an ice machine distributor, a company starting to grow. The owner had another business as well, and I was hired to work for both. For the first few years, Rod and I shared a cubicle. It was "cozy." As the company grew, the owner kept packing more and more equipment and parts into every available inch. Eventually, we grew enough for the owner to acquire the building across the parking lot. Ten years later we were able to build a building in a new industrial park and that's where the company is still today.

I worked there until I had Codey. I was able to stay home and be with him through the first year and a half of his life. The income source I had when Codey was born had dwindled dramatically since he needed all my time. By the time Casey was born, I was desperately trying to keep up my share of expenses. I cried out to God to provide a way for me.

When Casey was three weeks old, Rod called me unexpectedly to come back part-time to train someone they had just hired. She moved on and I wound up coming back full-time when Casey was three months old. When the boys were about four and five years old, I decided to start a house cleaning service so I could pick my hours and spend more time with them. I still went to help Rod with invoicing two or three evenings a week. God blessed me with as many cleaning jobs as I needed to accomplish what I wanted.

Once I knew my second divorce was inevitable, I worried again about finances. Yet, once again unexpectedly, Rod called and asked if I would come back full-time. I was able to work the same flexible schedule and receive the health insurance I would now need. I love how God provided in every case and I am so grateful to Him for caring so faithfully for me and my family.

I do believe that God has a plan and a purpose for each of us. My highest purpose and passion are family and caring for others, and God has been so good to me to provide fulfilling work that supported me financially and still allowed me to put my focus where my heart is.

Years later, I quoted ice machines for John over the phone. He'd call every month or so, but he and another salesman from his company sounded similar to me, so I couldn't even recognize his voice. I thought nothing of his calls. I certainly didn't have any idea that one day that guy and I would be married! I'm blessed to still be at the company (remotely) all these years later, which is a God story we'll dive into over the next couple of chapters.

Self-Reflection

During these years we were growing in our relationship with God. We started out following a religion—and one sign of this is the conversation John had with Jerry and Steve about what kind of baptism is correct. Of this kind of conversation, Paul says in Romans 14:17-18, "For the kingdom of God is not a matter of eating and drinking, but of righteousness, peace and joy in the Holy Spirit because anyone who serves Christ in this way is pleasing to God (NIV)." As our faith grows, we learn to study the Bible and gain understanding, and we're learning to remember Jesus simply tells us to love God and love others. We don't want to get hung up on differences that aren't salvation issues.

The more we go to God not only for our career choices but also for our choices and actions each day, the more we please Him—and the more we recognize His personal will for our lives. God has a plan and purpose for each of us. As we grow in our relationship with God, and especially if we are open to it, He will guide us to our purpose.

Like everyone else we asked ourselves "Life's Big Questions": "Who am I?" and "Why am I here?" If we place our identity in our work or what other people think about us, as we did, it's easy to go down the rejection trail. Our identity changes when we ask a different question: "Whose am I?" We are— we *all* are—children of God. Knowing this, we are learning to live *from* acceptance rather than *for* it.

- Where are you able to look back and see God teaching, using, and blessing you in your career? Where can you see Him working today? Give thanks to Him.

- Do you know what your purpose is? In what way are you fulfilling your purpose, God's plan for your life? What might you need to change to fulfill your God-given purpose?

- Describe a time when you worked as for the Lord. How did others benefit? Do you need to do this more? How will you?

*I wait for the Lord, my whole being waits,
and in his word I put my hope.*

—Psalm 130:5 (NIV)

Chapter 8

THE FLORIDA DISCUSSION AND THE WAIT

John's Testimony

In 2013, at thirty-four years old, I became general manager over fifty employees at a location selling $40 million worth of lumber and building materials. I was far enough along in my faith journey that I was able to give God the glory and thank Him for the doors He had opened. However, at that time, I expected Him to fit into my plans and bless them after I made the decisions, rather than asking Him for direction before I made the plans in the first place. God is merciful—I saw success despite myself.

My transition into this new position went well. Steve still worked at the same location and was there to train me. He supported me but let me take charge. He let me make mistakes and learn from them. However, I quickly realized I wasn't happy. I was trying to hit increased sales and profitability budget figures (and often did, but at the cost of much-added stress). There was a revolving door of employees at certain positions, including a driver that quit after two hours when he realized the hard work the job required. It wasn't uncommon to get someone fully trained on a forklift only to have them take their newly learned skills elsewhere. I felt responsible for each of the employees, so all this really got to me.

Every day there were fires to put out and I didn't know how I was going to be able to fix the situation. Yet there were days problems were solved, my confidence was boosted, and I felt like I could conquer the world.

As you might imagine, Donna wasn't a fan of my "little roller coaster."

When times were going well, I talked about wanting to move closer to my work. I was working a ton of hours and it would be much more convenient if we lived on that side of town. It would save me at least five hours a week. We weren't in a hurry, so we listed our house for sale by owner and were slowly completing repairs and improvements. A few people came and looked, but we never got any serious offers. I figured God's timing would eventually reveal itself.

One minute I would talk about buying a new house so I could be closer to work, and the next minute I was ready to quit that same job. I let the stress get to me so much that Donna finally forced me to go to the doctor because she was afraid I was having heart problems. I told her it was a waste of time given I had just finished a half marathon with no issues, but decided to do it to make her happy. I also couldn't deny I *was* having chest pains, struggling to breathe at times, and had other symptoms connected to heart issues. The tests showed no blockages, and the EKG came back normal; the doctor said my symptoms were caused by stress, not heart issues. "Maybe you should consider a vacation or a job change," he suggested.

I didn't take his advice right away, but by the spring of 2014, Donna and I were on vacation in Daytona Beach, Florida. "We should move here since we are both so relaxed," she said, laughing. Maybe she was joking but that got my wheels spinning. "If one of us could work remotely, we can do it," I said. "If we decide to do it, God will provide." In truth, I was putting more confidence in my own abilities.

We talked more about it with enough seriousness that we decided we should approach our bosses with the idea. Donna still worked at the ice machine distributor but by this point, Donna's brother-in-law Rod had semi-retired and his son, Mike, Donna's nephew, was her boss. Since he was family and more likely to be open to remote work, I convinced Donna to ask first. Of course, I knew I would–eventually–need to ask Steve. Donna and I and Steve and his wife planned to vacation together in Key West in a couple of months, and I decided to wait until then to talk to him about it. He would be relaxed and away from the work environment.

In addition to my work at the lumber yard, I already worked remotely. It was unusual for me not to work a little every night and on the weekends from home. I always took my laptop on vacation. On one "vacation" week, I worked forty hours dealing with multiple problems in the IT and accounting departments. . . . So much for a relaxing getaway!

Steve never forced me to do any of that. I lost count of the talks he gave me about needing work/life balance. I put more pressure and tight deadlines on myself than any boss ever could. Given all of that, if Steve was going to let anyone work remotely, it would be me.

Late one July morning in Key West on our vacation, Steve and I sat on the edge of the pool. With the clear waters of the Atlantic Ocean in front of us, we chatted and relaxed. Well, maybe Steve relaxed. Thinking about the conversation I wanted to start, I felt my heart beating fast as my nerves began to take control. I silently prayed, "God, please calm my nerves and give me the right words to say."

Keeping my gaze out on those clear waters, I mustered up enough strength to start the conversation. "Well, you know I have been stressed with everything going on with work. When we were in Daytona, Donna jokingly talked about moving to Florida. That got me thinking—and I don't know when, but I think we're going to do it. She has already talked to her boss, and she will be able to work remotely. What are the chances there would be a position that I could handle remotely?"

In typical fashion, Steve didn't answer immediately. After a moment he said, "John, I completely understand the stress you're having. I sat in that seat for twenty years, but we have big plans for you. I know it will get better. I want the best for you. I'd hate to see you throw away the opportunity you have in this career. While you no doubt would be responsible working remotely, you know I don't like remote workers and I have no intention of that changing any time soon."

Steve was a handshake, in-person type of guy and felt people hid behind texts and emails. Several times he had told me to pick up the phone instead of letting an email chain get out of hand. He stood firm that the answer to working remotely was no. He knew that meant I would look for another company to work for.

God knew I was impatient. The only way I wouldn't make a rash decision was by having a deadline. Steve was able to offer me that. He asked me to stay until the end of the year: the lumber company was going to be purchased by a national firm I'll call "Corporate." When the lumber company's owner had passed away, the company had put plans in motion to force the sale and not leave his family with the responsibility of running a company. I believe God put it on Steve's heart to ask if I would consider staying to help with the transition.

Corporate had been acquiring successful privately-owned lumber and building material companies where the owner was looking to sell. They wanted successful companies because they only had a small corporate staff and had no intention of replacing management or even changing the company name. It really was a good match. Steve pointed out that having a high-profile manager leave in the middle of the transition wouldn't be good for anyone. He also mentioned there may be more opportunities with Corporate after the acquisition.

Donna and I didn't know where in Florida we would move, let alone when, so I agreed to wait until the end of the year before I made any final decisions. The sale and transition with the company's new owners went well, and I told my employees that I felt the company sale was good for us. We'd have better health insurance benefits, vacation plans, and buying power, not to mention being able to learn best practices from similar companies across the country. Despite these plusses, by the end of the year the stress of my position didn't get any better, and the date I believe God set had come. It was time to talk to Steve again.

Donna's Testimony

The year before John took the general management position, I experienced the loss of my mother and my sister, Linda. In her 30's, Linda had developed Behcet's syndrome, a rare disorder that causes blood vessel inflammation. This disease is so rare that at the time, she was one of six people in the entire country who had been diagnosed. This disease often baffles doctors with its seemingly unrelated symptoms like Linda's: painful reoccurring mouth sores, skin rashes, lesions throughout her body, and loss of sight in her right eye. Her symptoms came and went, with no apparent reason.

She suffered for decades and was treated for things she didn't have before she found a doctor who could help. It took a trip to Mayo Clinic to find the correct diagnosis. It was a horrible disease with a horrible ending. The doctors told her she wouldn't live past fifty. But Linda threw her own fiftieth birthday party and then went on to live thirteen years longer! Along the way, her doctor started her on an experimental drug. As it turns out, the drug accelerated Alzheimer's. As bad as that sounds, the blessing was that her body "forgot" she had this disease, and she felt less pain. Toward the end, by the fall of 2012, Linda talked about Mom taking her home. Keep in mind that although our mom was still alive, we hadn't seen her in years.

Although my sister Linda's Alzheimer's was severe in her last year, during her last weeks, my sister Betty and I did have one last visit with Linda when Linda was aware of what was happening. She definitely recognized us and was speaking. We couldn't understand what she was saying, but tears were coming down her face. I said, "Linda, we don't understand what you are saying, but just know that we love you."

She clearly said, "I love you too." The day she died, just a week later, we were able to sit with her and talk to her and hold her hand. She passed away on December 15, 2012. She was sixty-three years old, the same age Dad was when he died.

Nearly two months earlier, on October 20, 2012, at eighty-six years old, our mom had passed away. She died alone while my stepfather, Jim, was out of town. We found out about it when he contacted my sister Carol a few days later. Her death was sad on so many levels. We really didn't know her; none of the grandkids knew her. Over the years, we all had reached out to her at one time or another, but she never responded, so she didn't know us either. It was reassuring yet so sad to learn about the life she'd made completely apart from us. Though Mom and my stepdad had a rough start—she was the reason for a lot of Jim's scars and missing teeth from back in the drinking days—they stayed married close to forty years. After those early years the drinking ended, and Mom became his whole world.

When my brother asked him what he'd loved about her, my stepdad said, "Her laugh, and her beautiful smile. She could light up a room! She loved to have fun and she was full of life." We found out there was a restaurant she and my stepdad loved and often ate there. A couple of the restaurant's waitresses loved her and came to the reception at the funeral home. They were shocked to learn she had kids and grandkids.

Right before Linda's death, I thought, "Wow, Mom may really be taking Linda home." Because those who knew her in her new life talked about how loving she was, I truly believe Mom found Jesus and turned her life around. I'm thankful for that!

Just months after all this John accepted the general manager position, along with all its stress. I knew he wanted to climb the corporate ladder, and everything seemed to be falling into place. He kept telling me all the long hours would pay off. Eventually, his stress level started rising. Not only did he have all the stress at work, but it usually took him an hour or more to get home afterward. What little patience he may have had after work was gone by the time he got home. Our house was only three miles from my work. But when he talked about putting the house up for sale and moving closer to work, I could certainly understand.

When we went to the beach in 2014, I *was* joking when I had talked about moving to Florida, or at least I was thinking we'd move in a few years, after I retired. We already had our house up for sale, so, best-case scenario, we would live close to where he worked and get a small place in Florida at some point. The next thing I knew, he was telling me if one of us could work remotely, we were moving. Now it was becoming real! John kept after me until I asked my boss, Mike, if I could.

The day I decided to ask, I was a nervous wreck. I felt pressured by John and was afraid of an uncomfortable conversation with my nephew that would end with him thinking I was crazy and telling me there was no chance of working remotely. I began praying. "Lord, I've been with this company for over thirty years. How in the world could I find a job that would be comparable to what I have?"

As I sat at my desk, I heard that familiar voice as clear as if I were talking to you right now: "It'll be okay; he'll work with you." Peace and confidence— just enough confidence to get me up out of my chair—filled me. I went to Mike's office, explained the situation John was in, and told him it appeared we would be moving to Florida at some point. It could be a year or three years, but we would be moving. I told him I loved working for the company and didn't want to leave. Would it be possible to work remotely?

Once again, I saw the hand of God, as my nephew informed me he'd recently started looking at new software that would enable us to work from anywhere! He assured me, "Sure, we'll work something out." This gave me peace of mind regarding my job, no matter what John decided to do.

I still had feelings to work through. I felt like John had put me in a vulnerable position and then changed his mind. With the new ownership at the lumber company, I did understand John's agreeing to wait until the end of the year. I wasn't convinced he was really going to leave. I knew Steve didn't want him to, and that weighed on him as well. I was glad the roller coaster had stopped for the time being, and John had a date when we would revisit the move idea. But I had no idea what was coming next.

Self-Reflection

It's easy to stress ourselves out and be on an emotional roller coaster when we try to handle everything without God. Life is busy, complicated, and we have lots of decisions to make. When we are in a season of waiting, when God doesn't seem to be answering our prayers, it can be even more stressful. But Holy Spirit can be our daily guide. John 14:26 says, "But when the Father sends the Advocate as my representative —that is, the Holy Spirit—he will teach you everything and will remind you of everything I have told you."

Over time we have both learned, and continue to learn, to go to God first. And of course, when we do, we have less stress and more peace.

More and more, we're realizing peace doesn't come from knowing every detail of the future or even having all the facts and figures today. We have peace with God through our Lord and Savior Jesus Christ. He gives us a peace that surpasses all understanding.

- How do you handle seasons of being in the waiting? How can you find more peace in believing that God knows what is best for you and this season has a purpose? Will you ask God, "Is there something I should be doing while I'm waiting? Is there something you want me to learn?"

- When faced with decisions, do you ask Holy Spirit for guidance? If not, will you commit to handling decisions differently moving forward?

- What is the root of your stress and lack of peace? Are you following God's purpose for your life? If you are, you will have stress, but you'll also have peace and joy. What changes will you make in your life?

The Lord isn't really being slow about his promise, as some people think. No, he is being patient for your sake.

—2 Peter 3:9a

Chapter 9

GOD'S TIMING

John's Testimony

Steve had invited me to attend a University of Louisville men's basketball game, and although I recall they trailed Clemson at the half, that first half was a blur as I was mostly thinking about how to start the conversation with Steve again about moving to Florida. It was January 7, 2015. We hadn't really talked about it since the previous July in Key West. Nothing better came to me, so I just blurted it out.

"I'm not sure how else to say this, but we're definitely moving to Florida," I said. "We need to figure out a transition plan to put someone else in my position." Steve still wasn't happy about the idea, but by this time a few other things were in motion. There was a manager at another location who wanted to move to Louisville and was very interested in my position. A former manager had left the company but was now looking to return. A transition plan couldn't get much cleaner than that.

The Corporate connection also helped because some of their staff worked remotely. Over the next few days, the lumber company's other branch managers caught wind of my plans and spoke up on my behalf. They knew I could help remotely, as I had helped them for years without physically being at their locations.

Steve slowly started to think something could work. He asked me to find out if any of the companies under Corporate's umbrella in Florida would be interested in "sharing me," since he wasn't sure there would be enough work from the lumber company for a full-time remote position. At the time there were only two companies in Florida and neither of them had any open positions. I told Steve if he couldn't commit to a full-time position for me, I would start looking for something else.

"Don't do that just yet," Steve replied. "I don't know what it will look like, but we'll figure something out."

Our house was still for sale by owner and hadn't seen much activity. The same week I told Steve we were definitely moving, we had three showings and an offer, which we accepted. If that's not God's perfect timing, I don't know what is.

The entire time I had had faith that God had a plan. However, when the house sold that fast after my finally putting a stake in the ground and saying the decision to move was final, my faith deepened. I suddenly had an unexplainable peace that the decision to move had been stamped by God. The worst-case scenario was a part-time position remotely for Steve that would allow me to move and then look for something else. I didn't know what the end result would be, but I was confident God had the details under control. I know now that the peace I had back then can only be explained by the presence of Holy Spirit.

Since our house was now sold, we had to figure out somewhere to live until we moved to Florida. Perry and Kitty, friends from the Catholic church we used to go to, had room for us. Their condo had a wing to itself that had a bedroom and a full bathroom. However, Perry was battling cancer. We were hesitant to ask but Kitty told us she would welcome the extra sets of hands to be with Perry and the extra income from rent would help as well.

A week before our scheduled date to move in, Perry lost his battle with cancer. This was now the second person from our close group from that church that passed away. (Our friend Judy had lost her battle with cancer a year earlier.) We rejoiced knowing they were with Jesus in heaven, but it was still tough. We told Kitty not to worry about us and we could find somewhere else to go.

Kitty insisted, "I want you to come now more than ever. After thirty years of marriage, I'm not ready to be alone."

We were extremely blessed to stay at Kitty's place during this transition period. This again was God's timing for us to be there for her as well.

Back on the work front things were falling into place. The other two managers had dates for their transitions, so Donna and I started looking for places to live in Florida. We had always heard the west coast was beautiful. Back in 2007, on our way to Miami to watch Louisville football in the Orange Bowl, we had spent one night in Sarasota, but we didn't get to see the area and had never been anywhere else. For reasons we would figure out later, I felt called to that area and decided to look for a church home first.

I put a spreadsheet together for churches from Dunedin down to Naples. (Who doesn't love a good spreadsheet?) I looked for their belief system, the size of the congregation, the outreach and small group offerings, and watched some online messages. There was a non-denominational community church at the top of my list, but there were other churches that had possibilities as well.

Donna and I had experience buying and selling houses without a realtor and didn't use one for this move either. We scheduled a long weekend in March 2015 to visit four houses and two churches. In the past, we had prayed for God to answer our prayers, almost like He is a genie in a bottle. Instead, this time, when we got in the car to drive down, we prayed for God's will to be done. "God, if this move is your will, let there be no doubt in our minds. When we walk into each house, let it be clear what we are supposed to do." He didn't disappoint.

We drove all night and were early to our first appointment in Dunedin, a suburb west of Tampa. It had advertised a private beach, so we decided to check it out. As we pulled into the complex, we noticed the area was run down: faded, peeling signs directed us through the area; deep potholes dotted the parking lot; and the "lawn" was more weeds than grass. We followed the signs to their beach and ended up in an area only forty yards long. It was muddy, and a few dead fish lay rotting on the sand—it looked nothing like the pictures. We could smell the stench of the fish even though our windows were closed. We canceled the first meeting without even seeing the condo.

The second condo involves another couple from our close group from the Catholic church in Louisville, Scott and Glenda. Scott's mom, whom we had met a few times, happened to live on the same street as the condo we were looking at. She loved her church and thought it would be great if we moved near her. We didn't end up buying that condo, but we had lunch with Scott's mom. To this day we still get together every few months with her. She has become part of our family.

I blame Donna for not buying that condo. I thought it was perfect. It was inexpensive and only two blocks from Indian Rocks Beach. Donna was NOT impressed. For some reason, she had a problem with the washer being in the master bathroom right next to the toilet, the dryer in an outside closet that required a hose to be run so the closet wouldn't get too hot, the low ceilings, or that it hadn't been updated since the seventies, including the avocado green refrigerator. She didn't care what the price was. She wasn't interested.

The third condo was in Palmetto, a small town about forty minutes south of Tampa. We were now getting to the area near the church I thought we would end up attending. This was a newer community on a small golf course. It was okay, but nothing spectacular. When we left, Donna said, "I'm looking for a 'wow,' and that wasn't it."

From there we planned on going to Saturday night service at Bayside Community Church in Bradenton, just south of Palmetto. Because I felt so strongly about God calling us to this particular church, this was one of the highlights planned for our trip. We had some time and were both tired, so we set an alarm and took a nap. We headed out, following the GPS, and it took us right to the old school the church had started at, not the new campus. We quickly adjusted the GPS, but now we were going to be a little late.

I *hate* being late. If I'm not fifteen minutes early, I get anxious just thinking about *potentially* being late.

I raced down State Road 70, doing 65 in a 50-mph zone. My attitude clearly was not the best. As I passed her, I even cussed out a poor old woman going 45. Donna stayed silent.

As we drove, I wondered if the GPS was misdirecting us again. As we'd say in Kentucky, the church was way out in the boonies. For a couple of miles before we arrived, all we passed were trees and meadows—and a few other churches.

Finally, we arrived. What was this place? The parking spots were grass. Smiling, waving greeters dotted the parking lot and stood at the doors just like our church in Louisville, but this church was significantly bigger.

We walked in the doors of the sanctuary and the music blew our hair back. It looked to me like the place could hold well over two thousand people and nearly every seat was filled. We ended up sitting in the back row of the balcony. All around us people were raising their hands in worship. How odd! The message was good, but we felt disappointed that the lead pastor we had been listening to online wasn't there. As we were leaving, we noticed everyone was happy. I thought, "That had to be fake." I was bummed. That church was at the top of my list and it just didn't feel right.

The next morning, we tried another church. It was okay but didn't feel right either. It was much smaller than our church back in Louisville and didn't have many outreach and small group options.

That day we had one more house to look at, in Bradenton. As we pulled up to the subdivision, we were surprised to see the community was gated. We didn't remember that from the ad, but it was a nice safety feature. The landscaping, construction, and even the street names reminded us of Key West: *Whitehead, Simonton, Duval,* and *Mallory Square.* We had been to Key West multiple times and by this point owned a timeshare there.

Our appointment was at a two-bedroom, two-and-a-half-bath townhouse. We fell in love with the community before we even walked in, and the inside sealed the deal. Upstairs had two suites with private bathrooms which would be perfect for company. Our office could be downstairs in an area separated from the open living room, dining room, and kitchen. The house had a two-car garage and a nice patio out back that could easily be enclosed. After we visited the community center, pool, kayak launch, nature trail leading to an island fishing pier and the marina, we were ecstatic. This would be like living at a vacation resort.

We didn't bother slow playing it. Less than an hour after we left, we called the seller's realtor with an offer, and they accepted shortly thereafter. The only part that didn't fall into place that weekend was finding a church home, but we knew God had a plan. We were confident we would plug into a local church.

The following weekend back in Louisville we mentioned to Brian, a friend at church, that we had just bought a townhouse in Bradenton, Florida, and would be moving soon. He said, "You have to try this church. My sister went there when she lived in the area and absolutely loved it." He told us the name . . . and it was Bayside Community Church. I felt as if God, through Brian, was reminding me this was the church originally at the top of my list. I told Donna we had to give it a second chance. It couldn't be a coincidence.

On the work front, Steve and I still hadn't finalized what my responsibilities would be working remotely. He told me it was a work in progress but guessed it would be forty hours. I had been working sixty to seventy hours and had management responsibilities and people working for me. My income would basically be cut in half, but this deal would get me to Florida. I listed out several additional tasks I could immediately help with remotely, and I knew Steve would be fair with my pay once the responsibilities were added. However, God wasn't done with His plan for me at the lumber company in Louisville.

Steve told me the company would soon be acquiring the competitor across the street and asked if I would commit to staying until July 1. That would be a big transition and he would feel better if I was on the team with boots on the ground for three-plus months. The Florida townhouse closing was tentatively set for late May, so, I figured, what's an extra month in the grand scheme of things?

That company's employees found out on a Friday afternoon their company was sold. We held interviews with them Saturday and Sunday, and Monday the employees we kept on arrived at work to begin using our point-of-sale software, one that was completely different from the program they had been using. I was trying to help all I could, but it was a madhouse. Plus, they had a lot more retail business than our company was used to, so I had many more people staring me in the face. Those were a stressful few weeks. Knowing I had an exit date in the near future helped, but I had an even more helpful strategy: prayer. Each morning before walking in, I prayed, "God, please give me the patience to deal with the storms that may come and the wisdom to make decisions throughout the day."

Adding to the stress of trying to merge two companies, several people quit during the transition. However, a core group stayed. I wasn't sure how they viewed me. I tried to squelch any "us versus them" mentalities. I hoped they recognized I was there to help and figured it didn't hurt they knew I was a short-timer. On my last day in Louisville, a few of the employees gave me a cake, a cheeseball (love those things), and a card with a restaurant gift certificate. It was a touching gesture, especially so since the gift certificate wasn't to a national chain. They had researched local restaurants in Bradenton and got one of those online. What started literally as a takeover ended being a group of people that sent me off in grand fashion. Little did I know that all of that was preparation for things to come.

Donna's Testimony

You may have picked up from John's testimony that he makes coffee nervous! He'd be up one minute, talking about moving across town and climbing the corporate ladder, and the next minute down on staying with the company, ready to uproot us and move to Florida. Unfortunately, my stress level was increasing based on his, and I couldn't be a part of that anymore. The only way I could deal with it was to take a step back. I told him, "When your roller coaster comes to a complete stop, I'll get on, but not until then. I don't want to talk anymore about whether we'll move to Florida or across town or what houses are on the market where."

Once he finally made up his mind about moving, I had to deal with leaving the only place I had ever lived. As I've said, I had fear and anxiety about anything new or different, and during this time, my fear was front and center! I was leaving my family, my friends, and my church home. And when we told our family and friends our plan, the reactions we were getting didn't help—they thought we were crazy. I felt so guilty, as if I were doing something wrong. I was even waking up at night, worried, praying and telling God what I was feeling. John was absolutely convinced that we needed to do this, but I wasn't feeling it. I told God I was stepping out in faith, and I was trusting Him to work it all out for our good. I told Him I didn't want to be a stumbling block for John if this is what He wanted us to do. It would still be a while before I heard His answer, and it wasn't the answer I expected.

Meanwhile, John went full steam ahead, and knowing his history of frequent moves, I could understand how he could pick up and go without even thinking about it. Once he made the decision to move, everything came together. I love how God works! I began to see how everything was unfolding just like God planned. Selling our house within days when John notified Steve—after it had sat on the market for over a year. Providing a place to stay for us in a way that helped our friend Kitty after she lost her husband. Even after we moved to Florida, we still came back to Kitty's one week a month for the next year due to my job. I was also able to see that John's leaving opened up opportunities for others that were in a perfect place in their lives to step into those positions.

I liked that John chose to look for churches first. That would've never crossed my mind. We loved our church, and as John said, we didn't think we would find another we would like as much. After his online research and prayer, John had initially felt sure he had found "the one." But you saw his reaction to Bayside. His attitude, coupled with the message, the music we could hear from the *car*, and all the people raising their hands in worship—for me, it was all pretty overwhelming. Coming from a Baptist/Catholic background, I had never experienced the joy the people at Bayside felt in a church. I thought we were just supposed to be respectful and somber.

I did, however, fall in love with the townhouse and the community immediately. That "Wow!" feeling I was looking for? I got it! The icing on top came when we moved in and discovered the development's little fifty-yard-wide island with the fishing pier at the end was called "John's Island." That was confirmation for sure.

When it came time to close on the Florida townhouse, we didn't even have to be there. The following weekend was Memorial Day. It would still be another month or so before John and I would officially move to Bradenton, but we figured this would be the perfect time to move our furniture to Florida. My younger son, Casey, was living in New York at the time, and we were flying him to Kentucky for the long weekend to celebrate his birthday. We decided to rent a truck and move most of our stuff while both boys were with us. They could help unload and see where we lived. That Friday after work John and a friend loaded up the truck, and John drove the rental truck down. Casey was arriving late that night, and Codey was working third shift, so I agreed to drive the boys down the next morning. It would be close to nine o'clock Saturday night before we arrived.

And when we did arrive, we had a surprise.

Yes, John decided to unload almost the entire truck by himself, rather than waiting for help. Remarkably, there were only a few casualties: some broken glass, two new holes in the stairwell, a broken TV stand, and some corners damaged on a dresser.

When we arrived John and the boys unloaded the last six big pieces . . . and we were done! That worked out great for us. We could relax and enjoy the rest of the long weekend. We went to the beach, and it was absolutely beautiful. The sand was powdery soft, the water was warm and crystal clear, and the waves were soothing for my soul. I'm so glad we had that time together as a family again.

Self-Reflection

Remembering how God's timing blessed and directed our move to Florida has been a big builder of our faith. We know we learned valuable lessons in this process. While we talked a lot about our options, we didn't *act* until we had a peace that God was directing our steps. We didn't force anything. For the first time, we asked to hear His will when looking at houses.

Something we learned through the writing of this book was how helpful it is to keep a prayer journal, in which we record prayers you have asked, including the dates. Then record God's answers to your prayers, again including the dates. Thinking about God's timing while we're waiting isn't a natural reaction. When it comes to waiting on God to answer our prayers or direct our paths, our patience can be pretty short. However, it helps to remember that in our waiting time God is often preparing us for what's coming next. He could be keeping us from trouble if we were to plow ahead, or delaying us because of skills or lessons we need to learn. God's timing is better than ours. Always.

- If you haven't already made one, start a prayer journal. You'll grow your faith as you review your prayer journal and note how God's timing benefited you.

- Have you prayed for God's will to be done in and through your life? If not, will you commit to that now?

- How much of a priority have you placed on finding a good church home? List what you are looking for in your church home—or what you appreciate about your current church home.

Perfume and incense bring joy to the heart, and the pleasantness of a friend springs from their heartfelt advice.

—Proverbs 27:9 (NIV)

Chapter 10

FRIENDSHIPS AND GETTING INVOLVED

John's Testimony

"Well, what did you think this time?" I asked Donna as we got into the car after church. As planned, we had given Bayside another chance after officially moving down in July of 2015.

It helped that we had prayed in advance for God to make it clear if this was to be our church home. Plus, we were able to sit where we usually sat at a church, near the front, because we had made sure we arrived on time. (Kipp early, meaning at least fifteen minutes before start time). We'd been listening to Christian radio stations, and this time we knew most of the songs. Having seen a service once before, we were more prepared for the differences between Bayside and our old church. This time, we came in with a different perspective and we felt happy to be there. Also, the lead pastor we had been watching online preached that week.

"I think this is it," Donna responded. And I agreed.

We were all in now. When we got home, we signed up online for a class to learn more about the church and to be on the greeter team, part of the church's "serve" ministry. The next week we received our blue serve t-shirts and brought them with us to the church introduction class. When he welcomed us, the lead pastor smiled and said it was the first time he'd seen someone already signed up to serve before attending the class to get to know the church.

At the time, we couldn't have verbalized what the difference was. Looking back, and after having been at Bayside for over six years now, we can confidently say what we originally saw as fake was people walking and serving with the joy of the Lord. Through this church, we have been blessed to get to know some of the most genuine and Spirit-led people we have ever met. They aren't perfect, but they understand what God's purpose is for their lives.

We were eager to get to know the people attending Bayside and form new friendships. I've been blessed with many friends over the years, and after moving so many times, I definitely was used to making new friends. Once I stopped moving and stayed in Louisville for eighteen years, the friendships grew to deeper levels than I had ever experienced. Years earlier when Donna and I had attended the Catholic church there, we had a core group we frequently spent time with. We'd often have dinner together on Friday nights and most certainly would be at lunch together after church on Sunday. We vacationed with them and even now that we live in Florida we keep in touch.

Many might think it would be impossible to find new friends like that, but Donna and I were confident God had some divine appointments in store for us. I signed up for a men's small group. For the first few weeks, I didn't say much, but the leader, Dale, saw something in me. Through his guidance and the work of Holy Spirit, within a year I went from a silent participant to a co-lead, then to a men's group leader. Most people now don't believe I ever would have sat in a group and not talked, but there was a time that staying quiet kept me comfortable.

Donna signed up for a women's small group and we signed up together for a class that taught the core principles of the Bible. Some of our closest friendships started from that group of about twenty people. A few weeks in, Donna was invited to a bunko gathering for women. Another couple invited us to dinner. The group leaders were pouring into us and encouraging us to co-lead with them the next round.

In a matter of weeks, this large church where we knew no one soon became small. Our greeter team served every three weeks. The first week we served, we didn't know anyone, but by the second time we served, we were happily greeting dozens of people we had met in the other groups. Many friendships had already started to form. It already felt like home.

Even though we were involved and in a couple of groups at church, I still thought about leading a small group at our house. The church started small groups three times a year, and at this point we were in between start times. Rather than wait to start an "official" group through the church, I thought it would be a good outreach to start something with our neighbors. I put up a sign at the clubhouse asking if anyone was interested in joining a small group Bible study. A couple of weeks went by, and no one contacted us.

I was about to give up when Jennifer emailed. She said her sister was visiting, saw the sign, and told her and her husband Kevin about it. (Jennifer and Kevin didn't frequent the pool and would have never seen it. God doesn't miss the small details that have to be put in place for His plans to work.) Jennifer and Kevin, who attended Bayside, were already involved in several groups and didn't have the bandwidth to add another group to their schedule, but invited us to a Bible study group they hosted at the community clubhouse once a month.

We decided to try their group and really enjoyed it. Kevin and Jennifer were fun to be with. They were outgoing, easy to talk with, and passionate about the Lord. They mentioned serving with a non-profit ministry that Bayside promoted, Feed My Sheep. Volunteers for Feed My Sheep took food bags door to door as a way to spread the love of Jesus. While that was a fabulous concept, walking up to a stranger's door was way outside our comfort zone.

A few weeks later our church had an outreach serve day to give away Thanksgiving meals. Along with close to two hundred others, we signed up to help. We didn't realize until we arrived that we would be distributing the meals door to door. Kevin and Jennifer had signed up to lead a team, and of course, we ended up on their team!

At the end of serving, Kevin and Jennifer gathered the volunteers back together and prayed over the group one last time. Then Jennifer said, "Bayside put this outreach together for Thanksgiving, but Feed My Sheep does this every Saturday, and we would love to have everyone volunteer next week."

Holy Spirit speaks to us all the time even if we're not paying attention. Sometimes He repeats things over and over until we get the hint. Donna and I recognized that God was directing us toward this ministry, and we started serving with them the following week.

We could write an entire book about our Feed My Sheep journey but here is the CliffsNotes version. We served every weekend for about three years;

during that time Kevin and Jennifer started serving somewhere else, but our friendship continued to grow. We became good friends with the founder of the non-profit, but he moved to Texas and we took over a leadership role. The food storage relocated to our house; more volunteers started participating, and we were developing some great friendships.

During our second year of this ministry, a new volunteer named Wendy joined our Feed My Sheep group. She is a true prayer warrior, and everything changed, including our prayers with the people who received the food. There was prayer before, but now it was different. We saw walls come down when Wendy prayed. The first time I experienced her impact was one Saturday when Wendy joined our group of three going door to door: Donna, one other volunteer, and me. We went to a woman's door and delivered the bag of food. We asked her if she wanted prayer and she said no. After a second, Wendy reached out, took the woman's hand, and looked her in the eye. Wendy opened her mouth and spoke words that only God could have given her . . . the woman was fearful that her sons were getting into drugs, and, a single mom, she also worried that she might lose their house. The woman saw Wendy's genuine love and desire to help and told Wendy more about what was happening. Wendy offered prayer and the woman said yes. Wendy then prayed, encouraging the rest of us to pray as well. We got used to people saying, through their tears, how much the prayers meant to them.

As one of the leaders, I felt my role was logistics. We wanted to get done in a couple of hours. If we had one hundred bags to prepare and hand out with twelve volunteers, then we had work to do. God gives us all different gifts, but I was Martha in a Mary's world (read Luke 10:38-42 for reference). It was normal for Wendy and Donna to stay at a door for fifteen minutes. One week, out of one hundred bags, Donna and Wendy only gave away *two* because they spent so much time praying and talking at each door. If we went to doors in groups of two and spent fifteen minutes at each one, it would take us over four hours to get done, which doesn't include preparing the bags! I would frequently "steal" Wendy and Donna's bags and pass them out myself so we could get done.

Eventually, Holy Spirit grabbed hold of me and helped me realize the importance of what they were doing. I could get things organized with the best of them, but at that time, as for the relationship-building side—well, there I was lacking. I learned so much while serving in that ministry. I learned, for example, that tasks, while important, are not what is most important to God. People are most important. God is in the relationship-building business. First, He wants relationship with each of us, then He wants us to have relationship with each other.

After several years, we stopped serving when it became an obligation. We felt the weight of the entire non-profit was on our shoulders. I said we, but if I'm honest, I let pride and stress come into the situation and then passed that on to Donna. I worried about weeks we would be gone and whether everything would get done. I was concerned what would happen to the ministry if we decided to stop serving. Having to purchase food, pick up donations, and keep everything at our house started feeling like chores that had to be done. As it turned out, God put other people in place to keep His work moving even after we stopped serving. The ministry was God's, not ours.

I discovered a couple of insights from this experience. First, if I'm serving in a ministry and it feels like an obligation, it may be time to move on. If I am serving in the area God has called me to, after "working" I may be tired, but I will feel more vibrantly alive, fulfilled, or "filled up" than when I got there. Second, if I think a ministry is going to fall apart if I stop serving, then I need to ask myself whose ministry it is, mine or God's? I've learned my pride can sneak into any situation. It's too easy for me to take credit for good results and forget about all the details and people that God put in place in order for those results to happen.

Leaving Feed My Sheep was a tough decision, but the ministries we were led to would change our lives forever.

Donna's Testimony

John did—and does—make friends easily. That wasn't the case for me. Making friends and getting involved in activities was daunting for me.

I knew most of the people in the Baptist church I grew up in, but back in Louisville when I first went to the Catholic church, I didn't know anyone. I just took the boys to church and then left immediately afterward. I purposely avoided making eye contact with anyone around me. Eventually, I did feel led to join the choir, and later I volunteered as a Eucharistic Minister, offering the communion wafers and cups to attendees during the church service. After the boys got old enough to play sports with their school teams, at games and practices I began to talk with some of the other moms. With them, I volunteered for the fish fries, the summer picnic, and fundraisers for the school. A couple of those ladies are still part of the core group John talked about, and we still get together whenever we are in Louisville.

After John joined the church, my circle of friends grew dramatically. John joined the choir as well and as cantor, led the congregation in the hymns during mass. He has a great voice and the church attendees participated more when he led. John also became involved with the school's social events and fundraisers—God certainly answered my prayer for a husband that would be involved in our church and the boys' school activities. John used to say he is not a people person. That was just a lie the enemy had told him to keep him from living out God's full purpose for his life.

Later, John was the same way with the non-denominational church we joined—he started out there knowing quite a few people, while I gradually met a few ladies through Bible study. This church also introduced me to the huge ministry Operation Christmas Child, run by Samaritan's Purse. I joined several ladies from my Bible study to go to the organization's shipping facility in North Carolina and prepare shoeboxes that would eventually go to a child somewhere across the world and show them the love of Jesus. It was a very humbling and rewarding experience. Our job was to make sure each shoebox was filled. We had a list of items that couldn't be shipped to other countries, such as liquids of any kind, food, breakables, and anything to do with guns or military—so no squirt guns. We would open the boxes and find bubbles, shampoo, candy, and fingernail polish and we had to pull all these out and replace them. Samaritan's Purse would then donate those pulled items to local charities. Some boxes we opened had the most beautiful handmade clothes with dolls to match and pictures and letters from families who painstakingly packed each box to overflowing.

As we put pens, small toys, socks, and other small items into the shoeboxes, something happened that inspired and awed me: the Samaritan's Purse team leaders stopped everyone so we could all pray over the boxes. This happened several times a day. Sometimes a volunteer spoke to the group about the impact they felt when they got one of the shoeboxes as a child. Once even Franklin Graham showed up to talk to us and give us a copy of his book.

Doing this kind of service with ladies from our church really strengthened our friendship.

After my first negative impression of Bayside Community Church, I only went back because John felt so strongly about trying it again. However, the second visit was a completely different experience for me. I think part of my reaction the first time was my discomfort about anything new. The second time I knew more what to expect, and it helped that the lead pastor, Randy Bezet, whom we'd been seeing online, was preaching. When we got back in the car afterward, I was excited and had no doubt that Bayside was our church home. Remembering John's initial reaction to Bayside, I was worried he would still feel disappointed. To my surprise, he felt the same way I did!

We got involved the very next week. I was so happy when we went from not knowing anyone on our first week of greeting to getting hugs from new friends the very next time we served, just three weeks later.

I was still struggling with leaving Kentucky. When we went back to visit, I would hear the comments. My brother Rusty said I had abandoned him. Friends asked, "Why would you go where you don't know anyone?" I backed away from some people because I felt like I had hurt them. I was so conflicted: I knew I was supposed to be in Florida, yet I felt like I had disappointed some family, friends, and coworkers. I kept praying about it and finally, after we'd been in Florida a couple of months, I got my answer. God told me, "I don't care where you live as long as you serve." That statement resonated with me. Yes, I had been active in the churches in Louisville, but had I really been serving? I had attended small groups and greeted people at the door. I had been staying in my comfort zone.

Once in Florida, I started praying for God to bring people into my life that would grow my relationship with Him. Next thing I knew, we (and by we, I mean John was going to have to drag me) started volunteering every Saturday morning with Feed My Sheep. We went to neighborhoods we weren't familiar with, knocked on the doors of strangers, offered them food, and asked if we could pray for them. There was NOTHING about it that was comfortable for me! I was scared of people, and they wanted me to knock on the door of a stranger? It was all I could do to hand them food, much less ask them if I could pray with them. It was so far out of my comfort zone that I would toss and turn the night before and wake up dreading to go. As it turns out, most people appreciated our being there, so each Saturday as the day went on, I ended up feeling so blessed to be a part of this ministry . . . until the next Saturday when fear set in again. But it was through the Feed My Sheep ministry I met Wendy. Talk about a direct answer to my prayer!

I had never met a woman so strong in her faith, so in love with Jesus. Wendy was from Australia; she had met her husband, a sailor from New York, when he was on furlough. So she could return with him to the U.S., they were married only about seven days after they met. Her Australian accent fascinated me. I could listen to her talk all day. But more than her speech, it was Wendy's gentle love that impacted me. She taught me to see people as Christ sees them, as His children. Wendy's prayers were effective. Besides the love of Jesus, Wendy also had some of Christ's boldness and Holy Spirit-inspired insight. One Saturday when I was in a group of five volunteers, we met a woman I'll call Rachel. Several times Rachel had fallen and she'd broken her wrist multiple times. Now she was unable to use her wrist, and kept it held up next to her chest.

As the rest of us stood in a circle facing Rachel, Wendy took Rachel's arm and prayed for complete healing for her hand. Immediately, Rachel straightened her arm and began moving her wrist. Her hand was healed and she could use it again! Rachel started grabbing and squeezing our hands, saying, "I had lost the strength to use my hand; I couldn't hold anything. I can feel strength in my hand—see? I can use my hand! My hand is strong!" She held out her arm, rotating her wrist, showing us she could move it. Rachel cried. We all cried.

A couple of months later, we were back on Rachel's street. We'd knocked on her door, but she didn't answer. When we finished for the day, we gathered with the larger group (probably fifteen to twenty people) in the parking lot for final prayer before leaving, and Rachel came over to pray with us. Rachel's hand was still healed. This time, Rachel asked for prayer for her back. We prayed for Rachel's back, and when we finished, Wendy asked, "Do you feel any relief?"

Rachel said no.

Led by Holy Spirit and in front of the entire group, Wendy asked, "Are you holding on to any unforgiveness?"

At first, Rachel said no. After the group broke up, Rachel walked over to Wendy and me on the side and said, "I am. It's my daughter."

Wendy led Rachel to forgiving her daughter and prayed again. This time Rachel felt immediate relief from the pain and stiffness in her back, and bent to the right, to the left, forward, and back, smiling and laughing with joy.

Wendy helped me to step out of my comfort zone. She would pull me into the conversation and ask me to pray. She showed me how important it was to spend time with people, and in doing so, I learned to see them differently.

I would love to say going out on Saturdays got easier and I looked forward to going, but that didn't happen. No matter how many Saturdays were filled with delightful encounters, I still dreaded going the next time. I now realize that experience was a steppingstone for what God had planned for me down the road.

Self-Reflection

We believe our number one friend is Jesus. But God wants us to have human friends as well. His Word holds many verses praising friends and friendships, like Proverbs 17:17a, "A friend loves at all times (NIV)," and Ecclesiastes 4:9, "Two people are better off than one, for they can help each other succeed." Whether you're married or single, the importance of having friendships can't be overstated.

Some may struggle to find friends. Others may have no problem making friends but are in the habit of surrounding themselves with people that aren't the best influence. In our experience, the best way to meet the *right* friends is in a local church. We went from knowing no one in an entire city to knowing hundreds in a short amount of time. What's the secret? Don't wait for people to come to you. We were intentional about getting involved and serving others.

That's what Jesus taught. The disciple Mark wrote of Jesus: "He sat down, called the twelve disciples over to him, and said, 'Whoever wants to be first must take last place and be the servant of everyone else'" (Mark 9:35). Serving brings people together. Most of our closest friends are those we have served with.

- How would you describe your closest friendships? Do they draw you closer to or away from Jesus?

- How are you serving others? If you are not serving at all, what potential areas could you be serving in? If you aren't now serving, what step will you take today to begin serving? Take this to God in prayer and act on what He tells you.

- Is there an area outside of your comfort zone that God could be directing you to serve in? Again, pray about this and see what God tells you. Then do that.

Therefore go and make disciples of all nations, baptizing them in the name of the Father and of the Son and of the Holy Spirit, and teaching them to obey everything I have commanded you. And surely, I am with you always, to the very end of the age.

—Matthew 28:19-20 (NIV)

And you will know the truth, and the truth will set you free.

—John 8:32

Chapter 11

FROM BAPTISM TO FREEDOM

John's Testimony

"**I** was baptized the day I was born. Why would I need to get baptized again?"

I've lost count of the number of times I've said this over the years. At the non-denominational church in Louisville we'd attended I had often felt a tug to get baptized again, but I never did it.

At their once-a-month baptisms, Bayside gives to those being baptized t-shirts that say "I have decided." At the baptism, the church pastor or leader explains this statement is "an outward expression for an inward decision." I felt uncomfortable with the "I have decided" concept. The way I was raised, newborns were baptized to remove original sin and receive Holy Spirit. There was no deciding about it.

Within a few months of moving to Florida, I changed my mind. I had wrestled for years over the many New Testament verses about baptism, like Acts 2:38, in which Peter says, "Each of you must repent of your sins and turn to God, and be baptized in the name of Jesus Christ for the forgiveness of your sins. Then you will receive the gift of the Holy Spirit." And Mark 16:16, where Mark quotes Jesus saying, "Anyone who believes and is baptized will be saved. But anyone who refuses to believe will be condemned." I had a lot of conversations with God about it and ultimately, Holy Spirit told me to do it out of obedience, so I did.

For me, it was a good experience, but honestly, nothing special. I remember thinking, "Okay, God, what's next?" I did feel moved to write my boss Steve and a few pastors from our Louisville church about it. They were encouraged to hear I made that decision and know their influence over the years had helped plant the seeds.

Fast forward a couple of years at Bayside to September 2017 when one of our pastors asked Donna and me to volunteer at Bayside's Baptism Weekend, where we'd be part of a team setting up the baptismal pool, outdoor tents, table with t-shirts, and guiding people into place. We said yes and joined the core group of volunteers, many of whom served after all three weekend services. We were shocked when, after we'd participated for just two months, we were asked to lead the team.

After a few days of thinking about it, we decided to say yes. Why? First, and most importantly, we prayed about it and felt God directing us down that path. Second, we were filled each time we served. We were able to witness people taking steps in their faith journey—and it wasn't just the person being baptized, but also the friends and family there to support them. We loved being a part of it. Finally, the team didn't have enough volunteers and we felt God might help us build the team. And He did. Because of all the small groups, serve teams, and outreach projects we had participated in, we knew a lot of people. God put on our hearts the people to ask, and we quickly went from a small team to three full teams of volunteers.

Shortly after, Holy Spirit spoke directly to Donna about adding something to the baptism event. From her time with Feed My Sheep, and by developing a deeper relationship with God, Donna had become a prayer warrior. When she said God told her to start praying for the participants one by one when they came out of the water, I didn't argue.

We needed more volunteers to pray, and God provided. Not only that, families and friends would join in the prayer. Our church had always made baptism a celebration, but prayer and giving thanks to God with each person makes it even more impactful.

We also started documenting the God stories from the weekends and emailing them to the volunteers and some of Bayside's pastors. One baptism had the observers—and both participants—crying when a young couple got baptized together. After exiting the pool, the man got on one knee before the woman and said, "We just made a public declaration that Jesus is our Lord and Savior and center of our individual lives, and I want to make another declaration that I want to spend the rest of my life with you. Will you marry me?" WOW! What a way to start a marriage.

During this time, we also started serving in Bayside's Freedom groups. Our church was transitioning from its biblical principles study groups (called Core) to Freedom small groups. The purpose of the Freedom groups was to develop the participants' relationship with Holy Spirit. We were honored to be part of the beta group testing out the material. The group met once weekly for seven weeks to discuss the lessons and watch a prepared video from one of the pastors. The finale was a celebratory weekend experience filled with worship, teaching, and prayer time.

By this point, we had been leading our campus' Core study group for a couple of years and loved it. We saw life change in those groups, particularly in the lesson about forgiveness. We were comfortable with the material and had the flow down for how to lead a group.

After going through the first few weeks of Freedom, I wasn't happy. Intellectually I understood the big point, that freedom comes with the presence of Holy Spirit. However, I was concerned this was going to be too deep for new believers. The study frequently asked the reader to write down what Holy Spirit was speaking to them. I barely even knew what that meant, and I had been going to church my entire life (as if that is a criterion for knowing Holy Spirit). Plus, how were we supposed to teach someone to hear from Holy Spirit?

I put an email together to the leader of our beta group explaining the problems I saw with the Freedom material and why Core was so much better. However, before clicking send I let Donna read it. She told me, "I don't see things like you do. This material and experience is life-changing for me. I've never heard from or communicated with Holy Spirit like I am through this curriculum." I decided not to send my email and see how the rest of the group felt.

The very next week the group leader started by asking what we thought about the material overall. Another guy started saying everything I had typed out in my email. I elbowed Donna and gave her one of those "See, I told you so" looks. Donna then gave that look right back to me when next a woman remarked she'd experienced the same things Donna had. How could the views be this drastically different on the same material? Was it the difference between men and women?

Nope. I would soon learn that I was going through the material trying to figure out how I was going to teach it. Donna was going through it asking God to speak directly to her as a participant. She was listening to and hearing from Holy Spirit like never before. It took me several months to realize this was not a class that had to be taught. We were supposed to be facilitators of conversation and Holy Spirit would be leading.

BUT . . .

"Filled with the Spirit."

"Baptism of the Spirit."

"Relationship with Holy Spirit."

In my Lutheran upbringing, I don't recall any of these topics being discussed. Before offering Freedom, Bayside held men's and women's weekends. I had heard Holy Spirit was a big part of the weekend but didn't really know what that meant. Donna went to a women's weekend, but I always had an excuse not to go to the men's weekend. Looking back, it wasn't God's timing because I would have attended with a skeptical point of view and likely would not have been a good influence on others.

When I first went to Bayside's Freedom, I wasn't comfortable with the way Holy Spirit was being talked about. (No surprise, right?). After the seven weeks of sessions, we attended Freedom Weekend. As always at our church, the teaching and music were powerful and moving. However, I wasn't comfortable with the ministry time when volunteers and staff were available to pray over us. We had multiple opportunities to be prayed over and I stayed in my chair each time. I was thinking, "I don't need anyone praying over me. I can take my concerns directly to God and don't need anyone else."

Freedom Weekend also included a segment when participants ask to be filled with Holy Spirit. During that time, it's common for some individuals to display manifestations that I had only heard about and certainly never witnessed—Someone might start laughing. Another might be overwhelmed with tears. One might end up on the floor. And another might start speaking loudly in tongues. Others may show no outward sign, but after prayer time would talk about what happened to them on the inside. Although I recognized that Holy Spirit could impact people differently when revealing His power, I judged what I saw as fake.

After the beta group was done, we were asked to co-lead a group. I wasn't fully on board, but Donna was all in and there was no stopping her. It was clear that God was leading her, and thankfully I wasn't stupid enough to go against that. That small group was okay, but I got in the way. When it was our week to lead, I tried to plan out the details of how the group would go from preparing the opening prayer, lining out which of us would ask what questions, to what quotes to share. I wasn't letting Holy Spirit lead anything. When that celebration weekend came, I once again stayed seated during prayer time.

Shortly after that group, we were asked to lead a group on our own. I still didn't feel ready, but by this point, I was hearing from God. Something different was happening and I wanted more of it. I was beginning to have conversational prayer with God and feeling Him lead my steps. Instead of praying in a more formulaic way, I found myself talking to God like He was a person, not some being up in a cloud. I'd say to Him something like, "God, I'm trying to serve you but I'm not seeing results." Or "God, you know I don't want to do this, but give me confirmation if this is your plan." I always got an answer . . . sometimes immediately, sometimes six months down the road. I was confident we were supposed to lead a group on our own.

To make ourselves more comfortable, we decided to load up the class with people we knew. This would only be the second session offered to the church as a whole, so most of our friends from Feed My Sheep hadn't been through the study yet. We ended up with almost twenty people, half of which we already knew. In an interesting twist, the other ten already knew each other—they all served in the kids' ministry and had decided to sign up together.

In preparation for this new group of people, Donna and I decided to do some things differently. Each week, we arrived arrive early and prayed over each chair and the room. Also, we wouldn't plan anything we were going to say—and, oh boy, was that hard for me. Finally, we ended each session with a worship song that God put on our hearts to play, which was the perfect ending each week.

By the time Freedom Weekend for this group came around, I had been talking to God a lot. I knew He wanted a closer relationship with me, but also realized I was a roadblock to that. I needed His help. I went up for each of the prayer opportunities and was blessed each time. At one point, one of the prayer team prayed for God to help me surrender and release control. I didn't realize I had my hands closed into fists until I clearly felt my hands relax and open, palms up, into "receive mode." As the volunteer prayed for me, I could feel Holy Spirit release the tenseness I had walked up with. I was finally starting to understand what Freedom meant, and it wasn't just others that needed it. I was thrilled that Donna had brought me along on this journey and was excited that we would have more opportunities to help others find freedom.

Also about this time, in the fall of 2017, one of the other leaders asked me if I had my prayer language. She said that a prayer language is praying in a tongue not recognizable to us. She explained, "This isn't the gift of tongues talked about in 1 Corinthians 12:28 where one person speaks and another interprets. It's a personal prayer language between you and God." She read to me Paul's words to the Corinthians, "For if I pray in tongues, my spirit is praying, but I don't understand what I am saying. Well then, what shall I do? I will pray in the spirit, and I will also pray in words I understand. I will sing in the spirit, and I will also sing in words I understand" (1 Corinthians 14:14-15).

Again, I wasn't comfortable with this concept. However, the people I knew who had this gift seemed to have a connection to God that I didn't. I have always struggled with wanting control, and letting go of control of my tongue was even scarier to me. One day, I decided to talk to God about it. I told Him, "If this is real, and is a gift you desire for me, then I want to receive it." And then it happened. I spoke something I didn't understand. I didn't know if it was one word or a phrase, but I had a peace that it was definitely Holy Spirit speaking through me. I had a sense that I was praising God at a level above saying Hallelujah. This explanation doesn't do the experience justice. For those that have experienced something similar, you will understand. For those that haven't, and you just decided I am some kind of weirdo, I get it. For now, please just agree Holy Spirit does things that we either can't see or can't understand at the time and continue reading.

Donna's Testimony

When we were asked to help with baptism, I was excited about it. For me, baptism had always seemed mysterious, joyful, sacred. At the Baptist church I grew up in, the baptismal was behind the choir, hidden behind a curtain. We didn't have a set weekend for baptism each month. When a person went up for the altar call to receive Jesus as their Savior, baptism would follow a week or two after. Usually, baptism would happen at the beginning of the service: The curtain would open, and the pastor would be standing there ready to receive those being baptized. After each person came up out of the water, the congregation would erupt in celebration! No matter what church we have attended, baptisms always meant celebration.

We didn't know what was involved in putting baptism weekend together at Bayside, but we knew that the baptisms were outside. How cool is that? The setting was a beautiful grassy area with three crosses in the background. For families, friends, and anyone else who wanted to witness the celebration, we set rows of chairs out on the grass facing the baptismal pool. There were also tents for changing rooms, a check-in table, and music. We offered shirts, shorts, and towels for anyone needing them. The first time we helped and saw the joy of those being baptized, I was filled with that same joy! I knew I was meant to serve in this ministry. It wasn't long before I heard God say, "Pray for them" as a group. I understood that prayer was needed, not just for the people being baptized, but for those who came to support them as well. God wanted them to pray together to create a bond of joy and commitment to each other. I saw that it was God's heart for the family and friends of those getting baptized to know they were part of the journey.

About Core—yes, we loved being involved in Core and meeting new people. With each Core group, God continued to bring more friends into our lives. Our pastors often said, "Relationships happen in the context of small groups," and it was really true.

The Core book we used had "fill-in-the-blanks" statements for each lesson. Oh, how John loved those! He filled in every blank ahead of time during the first group we attended. People took turns reading parts of each page and then we would talk about the concepts. Our leaders knew what questions to ask to draw all the attendees into the conversation. I wasn't used to talking in a big group, so I didn't say much. Sure enough, each week the leaders would ask: "Donna, what would you like to add?" As uncomfortable as that was, it did help me to open up some. On the surface, I was pretty happy. I felt like I had left the past behind and was moving forward; I saw no reason to look back. But God had other plans.

My relationship with Holy Spirit deepened at Bayside's Women's Weekend. As Pastor Kim prayed for me during Holy Spirit time, she said the words, "You are His baby girl!" How could she have known that had been my prayer!?

The Women's Weekend went from Friday night to Sunday afternoon at a retreat center about an hour and a half away from our church. A friend of mine, Tori, asked me to go with her. I'm always up for a road trip so I said, "Sure!" I had heard from other ladies about what a wonderful experience it was, though I really didn't know what to expect.

Each session at the Women's Weekend started with worship, then a topic such as life wounds or generational sins. Next, we had a breakout session, eight ladies and one of the leaders, going more in-depth. We also had time alone as well, to pick a place on the peaceful, rural property to pray and meditate.

One breakout session in particular stood out to me. In that session, which focused on life wounds, I was amazed to hear that every lady in our small group had experienced some kind of abuse as a child. I had thought my situation was rare. Instead, it appeared to be common, but just not discussed.

The next session focused on Holy Spirit. When I was young, the only concept I had about Holy Spirit was during baptism when my Baptist pastor would say, "in the name of the Father, the Son and the Holy Ghost." By this point in my life, I had a growing awareness of Holy Spirit, but not what I would call a relationship. To be honest, I can't remember a thing said during the session, but when the leaders went up front, offering to be prayer partners for us, I was moved to go and ask to be filled with Holy Spirit. As Tori and I stood in line, I was crying uncontrollably for no reason evident to me. I had told Tori the story about the Angela Thomas Bible study, "When Wallflowers Dance," that I shared earlier in this book. In that study, Angela talked about being God's baby girl. I told Tori how cool it would be to hear God tell me that. I went to Pastor Kim as my prayer partner, and she said those exact words.

I couldn't help but wonder if she had somehow heard me (way back in line, in a crowded, noisy room), but ultimately, I knew Holy Spirit had spoken directly to me through her. After it was over, I asked Pastor Kim to explain what happened. How did she know to say that? Did she hear directly from God? Why was I crying for no apparent reason? Could she see Him? She said that when we open our hearts and minds and ask Holy Spirit to speak to us, amazing things can happen.

WOW! Pastor Kim really got me thinking in new ways about Holy Spirit. She told me Holy Spirit loved me and He wanted me to trust Him. "Trust Him for what," I wondered. There is no doubt that I felt Holy Spirit that day. However, I didn't know what to expect or how to react to Him until Freedom.

When I heard the word "Freedom," I was surprisingly moved. I knew nothing at all about the study, but somehow I knew I needed it! The study's introductory words themselves grabbed me: "Freedom is not the absence of someTHING, but the presence of someONE—Holy Spirit." I have talked before about the quiet voice or hearing from God. That was the voice I had heard the day I was baptized! I finally realized it had been Holy Spirit speaking to me my whole life, convicting me, protecting me, and never leaving me. Now I not only knew He was talking to me, but I also knew I could talk with Him!

I don't completely understand how the Trinity works, but I'll always remember what John's dad told me about it, "We are calling upon the true God (Trinity) when we pray. We are speaking *to* the Father, *through* the Son, *by* the power of the Holy Spirit."

Through the Freedom material, I began to understand the love of God. As a mother, I love my boys unconditionally. I would lay down my life for them. I didn't see God that way until going through Freedom. I realized God loves ME that much and more. Jesus loves ME! Holy Spirit loves ME! As the Freedom group went on, I knew I was going to have to go back and unpack all the ugly in my life. God didn't want me to bury it. He wanted me to face it, with Holy Spirit's help. What I had experienced was part of my story; facing it would bring healing. Holy Spirit took me back to my earliest memories, and little by little, like peeling layers from an onion, walked me through my past. As I read the Freedom content, I would feel His presence and cry uncontrollably. They were tears of healing and release as I relived situations and then gave them to Jesus. At times like this, I would go to my "war room" prayer closet, sit on the floor, and talk to Him. I would become that scared little girl again. Where was God when I cried out to Him? Even though I couldn't see Him, I knew, somehow, He had seen me then and cried with me. He saw me now and cried with me.

By the time I reached the weekend sessions, I had already been dealing with underlying issues such as fear, rejection, bitterness, and self-centeredness. The study provided tools to overcome those issues, replacing fear with faith, rejection with acceptance, bitterness with forgiveness, and self-centeredness with God-centeredness. If that weren't enough, the weekend session helped me deal with generational sins, soul ties, and life wounds. I saw how history had repeated itself in my family (generational sins), how hurts and trust issues from my past marriages were still following me (soul ties), and how others' words and actions had damaged me (life wounds).

Freedom Weekend includes these questions: Ask Holy Spirit what is the lie you are believing about God and what is the truth? And, what is the lie you believe about yourself, and what is the truth? One of the lies I believed about God was He wouldn't forgive me for what I had done. The truth was, I was already forgiven even before I was born, because of what Jesus did for me, not by anything I did. God loves me unconditionally and I can come *to* Him; I don't need to run *from* Him! The lie I believed about myself was I had no control over the negative thoughts that came into my head. The truth is my identity is in Jesus and I wasn't defined by my past. I could replace the negative thoughts with the truth of who I am and *whose* I am!

If you've been reading along in this book, you know that fear had been paralyzing me since I can remember—it's one of my life wounds. The spirit of fear had held me captive and kept me from really experiencing life. The fear of people, of the unknown, of being alone, of being ridiculed, of flying. You name it, I feared it.

When we were leading our first Freedom group, John started traveling for work. That left me leading the group by myself from time to time. John and I had been together 24/7 since we moved to Florida. Now, I found myself alone some nights. We had a townhouse, and our bedroom was upstairs. When John was gone, I could not make myself go up there. There was only one way out and I felt trapped. Even if I never left the house the whole day, once it got dark, fear started creeping in and, by bedtime, I just knew someone was coming to hurt me. I could actually feel someone behind me ready to pounce. Even the hair on my arms would stand up, so I would stay downstairs and sleep on the living room couch until John came home.

One night when John was gone, I went to a Freedom volunteers' meeting. The staff member leading the meeting mentioned fear and this verse: "For God has not given us a spirit of fear and timidity, but of power, love and self-discipline" (2 Timothy 1:7). Wow! The spirit of fear was a living, breathing spirit but Jesus gave us authority over fear. That night I went home and—it took all I had, but I did it—I went upstairs. In our bedroom, I looked in the mirror and knew there was nothing behind me, but the hair on my arms still stood up and I could feel someone behind me!

That's when Holy Spirit said, "Yes, there is a spirit of fear, but I am a Spirit too and I've got you." I finally understood that through my fear I was giving the enemy control over me. I didn't want Satan to have any part of my life, so I talked with Holy Spirit, and He revealed the root of my fear was the fear of death. He walked me through the scenarios I was imagining, and I knew I had to trust Him with my life. I had no control of what would or could happen to me, but I came to believe that whatever happens, He's got me. That night I received His peace and a new perspective of His love and protection. I was also able to share this experience with our group. That brought extra blessing when I saw that, yes, facing what I had experienced would help me heal—and sharing it would help others heal.

Self-Reflection

Freedom isn't the absence of someTHING, it's the presence of someONE. That simple statement may not have sunk in for you yet. We are still learning what that fully means and growing our relationship with Holy Spirit. One of the ways to do that best is through God's Word. We encourage you to dive into the Word and ask God for your eyes to be opened and your heart to be willing to receive all that He has in store for you. The relationship He wants to have with each of us is greater and more intimate than any of us can imagine.

- Baptism is an outward expression of an inward decision made from the work of Holy Spirit. Have you been water baptized? If not, what is holding you back? After hearing the Word of God, will you commit now to being baptized?

- Do you have a relationship with Holy Spirit? Does that relationship help you to live a life in freedom? If not, what steps can you take to develop the relationship?

- How do you define freedom? Have our testimonies changed your perspective in any way? How?

Keep on asking, and you will receive what you ask for. Keep on seeking, and you will find. Keep on knocking, and the door will be opened to you.

—Matthew 7:7

Chapter 12

THE KNOCK
AT THE DOOR

Donna's Testimony

"**M**rs. Kipp, your results were abnormal, and we need you to come in for more tests," the nurse told me over the phone. I'd had mammograms for years with absolutely no issues. I went for my first mammogram in Florida on December 22, 2017, and they found something. The nurse made me a follow-up appointment for exactly one week later.

I kept my focus on Christmas week and decided not to think too much about what might be going on with me. Maybe I was in denial, but I know I felt an unexplainable peace. When Dec. 29 arrived, I woke up and prayed. I was surprised when the prayer that popped out of my mouth wasn't even about my health. I prayed, "In Your timing, bring us a house we can use to direct more people toward You." This was a frequent prayer for me at the time.

We loved living in our townhouse but wanted something bigger so we could host groups. All the groups we led had been at church or in someone else's home. We would occasionally look online but we really didn't want to leave our community. There were a few houses in our complex, but they rarely became available. In casual conversation one day I had mentioned our interest to our next-door neighbor, Jack, but didn't think it would lead anywhere. After my prayer time, off to the appointment I went.

I spent at least two hours at the diagnostic center. They took scans, and I waited for the results; they took more detailed scans, and I waited for the results; then they gave me an ultrasound, and I waited some more. The longer it took, the more anxious I was feeling. Eventually, the doctor said the results were inconclusive, so they wanted me to come back in six months. As I left, I asked Holy Spirit to give me confirmation that I was going to be okay.

When I got home, I told John about my ordeal. He didn't have much to say—and then, surprisingly, he asked, "You want to go look at a house?"

A little shocked, I responded, "Uh . . . sure. When?"

He said, "Let's go now—we can walk there. Jack knocked on the door while you were gone and said some friends of his, who lived a couple of blocks over, were ready to sell their house. He remembered our mentioning that we would like to move into one and thought we might still be interested." As he spoke John was moving quickly, closing up his laptop, putting papers away. I could tell he was excited. He continued, "They haven't listed with a realtor and were hoping for a quick sale by owner. They have already started construction on a new house and said we could come look at it any time."

I knew in my heart that was confirmation, for my diagnosis as well as the house. Sure enough, the doctor continued to monitor me every six months for a couple of years. Nothing showed up, and I was able to go back to the normal mammogram schedule and have had no further problems.

We looked at the house and it was perfect, exactly what we'd prayed for. We would have room for our office, plenty of space for groups of twenty in the open living/dining area, and we'd remain in the same community. We were able to agree on a fair price with the sellers, but there was one problem. They were looking to close quickly and had no interest in a contingency contract. To John, it made no sense to sign a contract before our townhouse was sold and end up with two payments, but I believed we should step out in faith.

I was convinced our townhouse would sell and prayed it would happen before we made the first payment.

One morning shortly after we closed on our new house, someone was coming to see the townhouse, so I was getting ready to leave to go shopping with a friend. Before I left the house, I heard Holy Spirit say, "You will get a contract." I was so excited. . . . But the people came and looked and no offer.

I felt disappointed and confused. Had I misunderstood? I knew I had heard from Holy Spirit. . . . Apparently, I added "today" to what Holy Spirit told me.

A couple of weeks later, while John was out of town, he prayed we'd get an offer before he came home. And just like that, we received an offer, and signed it right away! However, it turned out the couple that made the offer had actually first made an offer on *another* townhouse in our community. The couple told us their offer on our townhouse was void. Maybe we could have fought the issue, but we chose not to. Still, I couldn't understand why Holy Spirit would tell me we would get a contract and then pull it away. I had enough sense to know it was not in God's nature to treat me that way, but I felt anxiety coming as our first payment was around the corner. Holy Spirit helped me realize we were praying for our timing, not God's. We would get a contract in God's timing. That completely changed my perspective. I began instead to pray for protection and provision until His timing was revealed.

When I talked to people about our reasons for moving, I often mentioned the townhouse's staircase, explaining, "It's difficult for some of our older family members." Every time I said this, I heard Holy Spirit say, "It's for *you*." That puzzled me—was I hearing correctly? I had no trouble with the stairs. Little did I know what was coming next. . . .

John's Testimony

When we first moved to Florida in 2015, we made a leap of faith. I took a drastic pay cut, and, to most people, our decision didn't make sense. On the work front, a miracle happened quickly, though. After we'd been in Florida for only two months, the company made an overnight decision to replace the president and Steve would now be in charge. He was ready for me to move back and help but he knew I was loving Florida. Plus, I knew Eric, the current controller, should be vice president. He was a good leader that truly cared about people. I was glad for him and it opened the door for me to take back some of the controller responsibilities. Eric knew I could handle the work remotely with just a few changes to the position. I went from moving with a pay cut and not knowing what my job was going to look like exactly, to being the controller again, loving all of my responsibilities, and having my salary restored to nearly what it was before the move. God is good!

Fast forward to December 2017. The knock on the door and the house being available was certainly a God-story, but it still made no sense to me to have two house payments. However, Donna's confidence that God was working and her reminder that He had taken care of us before was enough that the least I could do was find out if the bank would even give us a loan without our townhouse being sold.

The bank approved us for a loan that had the option for a one-time recalculation of the payments once we sold our townhouse. I couldn't believe we were doing it, but we signed the contract and had a closing date for March 2018.

In typical fashion for us, we put our townhouse up for sale by owner. We had some immediate interest but no offers. There was a steady flow of showings, so we stayed encouraged, but it didn't sell by the time our new house closed.

In God's perfect timing, the first Freedom small group we would host in our new house was scheduled on the day of the closing, March 29, 2018. Even in the midst of the uncertainty of a closing (where sometimes glitches do happen and deals do fall through), we saw this was an example of God's timing, and we weren't stressed. Instead, we were excited. Everything went as planned. We had nothing in the house except a TV stand (still in the box), a TV to show the video, and folding chairs. We asked the group to stay afterward and help pray over the house. I don't think there could have been a better way to start this new adventure.

People still showed interest in the townhouse, and we showed it about once every other week, but after a couple of months, doubt crept into my mind. Had we really heard from God, or did we make a decision—a costly decision—we would regret for years to come? Should we hire a realtor? Should we lower the price? I even tried to bribe God: Our church was having a donation drive to raise funds for a new campus launch, and I told Donna I felt we should give early. What I didn't tell her was I was thinking God would bring a buyer sooner if we did.

Well, it didn't work. God knew my heart and He doesn't work that way. Phil 2:3a says, "Do nothing out of selfish ambition or vain conceit (NIV)." We are big believers in tithing, and even though I knew I shouldn't be doing selfish deal-making with God, I had given in to my doubts. I apologized to God, telling

Him I knew our giving should just come from our hearts, without strings of self-interest.

In late May, we finally received a good offer. However, it had a contingency on the buyers selling their house. They were asking a reasonable price for theirs and it looked ready to sell, so we accepted the deal and gave them sixty days. Right after signing, I told Donna I didn't think the deal would go through. Something was telling me this was just like the waiting I did before moving to Florida. I sensed that God had something planned, and because He knows the way I'm wired, He brought this contract to give me sixty days to chill out. I couldn't agonize over changing the price or hiring a realtor; I could only wait. So, we entered this new waiting period. In contrast to me, Donna was at peace the entire time, from the day we looked at the house to the closing on the townhouse months later. Yes, we did eventually sell the townhouse, but a whole lot happened before we did.

Self-Reflection

God doesn't only want us to believe He exists. He wants us to have faith in Him. And He doesn't only want us to have a little faith. He wants us to have deep faith, BIG faith. As Proverbs 3:5 says, "Trust in the LORD with all your heart and lean not on your own understanding" (NIV). God jealously desires YOU.

Of Abraham, Moses wrote: "Abram believed the LORD, and the LORD counted him as righteous because of his faith" (Genesis 15:6).

And the apostle John, the disciple "Jesus loved," wrote that Jesus said to Thomas, (the doubting disciple), "You believe because you have seen me. Blessed are those who believe without seeing me" (John 20:29).

Taking a leap of faith isn't the focus here. If we talk to God about decisions in advance and listen for an answer, God is part of the process and the leap doesn't seem as big. When we take time afterward to reflect back and see Him in the details, remembering all the answered prayers builds our trust in God. Doing this is how we grow our faith.

- Have you made plans that would be considered a leap of faith? What happened? How did God work out the details? We recommend you write your prayers, leaving space for God's answer.

- Describe what it is like when you are confident you are hearing from God. If you have never experienced that, ask Holy Spirit to open your heart and ears to have the confidence to know not only that God speaks, but that you can hear Him.

- Make a point to pray before you make plans today. Even if it is something as simple as where you are going to have dinner, ask Holy Spirit to direct you. Afterward, reflect on what happened. Did God show up? How?

And the Holy Spirit helps us in our weakness. . . . And we know that God causes everything to work together for the good of those who love God and are called according to his purpose for them.

—Romans 8:26a, 28

Chapter 13

THE ACCIDENT

Donna's Testimony

Tuesday, July 17, 2018.

It was the most amazing fall. In fact, pretty much nearly everything about the accident was amazing.

John and I, along with six of our old Louisville friends plus some of their family members, were staying in two condos in Key West for a weeklong vacation. I'd been working in our condo the morning of that sunny day and had just arrived at the large outdoor pool area.

Centered on one long side of the pool was a patio section, located slightly lower than the pool and filled with two rows of lounge chairs. That's where our group was. John and a couple of the guys were in the pool, and the rest of the group was relaxing on the chairs. Between our chairs and the pool was a slight incline covered with natural slate. A row of low scalloped concrete edging pavers, just a couple inches off the ground, separated the bottom of the slate incline and our lounge chair area. We could get to the pool by going up the incline or using the steps located on either side of our patio section.

As more people got in the pool, the water would rise, and a bit of water would overflow onto the slate and down into the area where we were sitting. If we weren't careful, anything we had on the ground would get wet. That also made the incline area a little slippery.

I took a float and walked up the incline to get in the pool, but too many people were lined up at that side of the pool for me to get in. I turned and started to walk up the steps, but there were too many people there also. When I started back down the steps, I saw there was now room for me to get in the pool by going up the slate incline. From a step close to the bottom, I extended my right leg over the scalloped border. When the ball of my right foot touched the surface, my eyes closed, involuntarily, and all I could see was a pink background.

My first thought was, "Well, I can't see where I'm going, so I'll just stand here."

Then I felt a little embarrassed wondering what people were thinking of me just standing still. I heard Holy Spirit say, "Remember the color pink." I felt a tug and heard a bone pop. I felt no pain, but I told God, "I just broke my foot on vacation; I can't believe I just broke my foot on vacation!" I thought about the people we were with, and how this was going to change things. I thought about having a cast and envisioned what that would be like. I had never broken a bone in my life and had no idea what to expect. The realization of what just happened was sinking in, yet I felt overcome with a powerful sense of peace that everything was going to be fine.

In my mind, I was still standing. I still couldn't see anything, so I said: "Okay, God, at least let me see it."

Instead of facing the pool, I was already on the ground, on my back on the slate incline facing the scalloped border wall. My right leg was in the air and my foot wasn't where it should be. I could feel my left foot throbbing. I sat up and saw my left foot was under the scalloped border. I slid it out—the top of that foot was already swelling and bruising. I never felt a sensation of falling, yet I was on the ground. My left foot had been on the steps when I stepped over the border with my right. How did I have enough force to bring my left foot across, turn my whole body around, and reach the concrete border with both feet?

Though the pool area was packed, no one saw me fall. I was sitting up, looking at my foot, when I heard someone from the direction of the pool say, "Hey, that lady broke her foot!"

Within seconds, a woman came to me with a bag of ice. "I'm a nurse," she said. She knelt beside me, and, with a voice both gentle and firm, said, "Lie down." Moving quickly, she put the ice bag on my right ankle. (Crazy that a nurse was right there, huh? A nurse who just happened to be carrying a bag of ice. . . .) One of our friends, Scott, a retired police officer, was already on the phone calling 9-1-1. Another of our friends, Kitty, came over and she and Scott held a beach towel over me to give me shade. Key West, midday, July—it was humid, of course, and probably 90 degrees. John was coming to me, but Scott told him to run and get my ID and insurance card. John spun around and ran.

In just a few minutes the ambulance arrived and two EMTs carrying a stretcher and a supply bag hustled over to me. One of them knelt beside me and asked, "Are you in pain?" He had brown eyes and a nice smile. I told him my left foot was throbbing, but that was it. My right foot was just dangling, and a bone was about to come out of my skin, but I didn't feel anything. The EMT held his fingers to my right ankle for a few seconds. "I'm not getting a pulse," he told his partner. Then he turned to me and said, reassuringly, "Don't worry about it, that happens." Next, he asked what seems to be a common question for accidents in Key West: "Have you been drinking?"

I assured him I hadn't.

What a picture: me being lifted up on a stretcher by the pool, (nothing to see here) and taken by ambulance to the hospital in Key West.

Once John and I were in the ambulance, Brown Eyes checked my blood pressure: 98 over 60. He looked at the gauge again, then at me, head cocked, assessing. He asked, "Is that your normal blood pressure?"

I said, "Pretty close, yes."

He looked at me again, looked at my foot, looked back at me, and asked, "Are you an athlete?"

After I finished laughing, I said, "Uh, no." He couldn't believe my blood pressure wasn't elevated after what happened. The peace of the Lord is my only explanation.

Scott and his wife Glenda followed us to the hospital, which was pretty small. The EMTs wheeled me in, right past the check-in desk and little waiting area into one of their two curtained rooms. The one I was in doubled as a storage area. The bed was at one end and at the other end was a storage cabinet full of blankets, what looked like a portable x-ray machine, some I-V poles, cords, and some heart-rate monitor machines. The whole time I was there, nurses and aides kept coming in to get blankets and other supplies.

Within minutes, a nurse came in. As part of the report she was getting, she asked me, "Have you been drinking?" The doctor soon followed. He asked me a few questions, including the drinking one.

The doctor ordered an X-ray of my right foot. Glenda piped up, "I think you should look at the left one, too."

"Why? I really don't think we'll find much there."

Glenda persisted. "Donna said the only one hurting was her left foot."

He ordered both X-rays. He held his fingers to my right ankle, feeling for a pulse. Nothing. Then he moved his hands over my right foot and ankle. "Okay, we're going to set this thing back," he said. I found out later that the doctor was waiting to find a pulse before he would set my break. Thank God, he finally did. No pulse would have meant an even worse injury and possibly emergency surgery to restore the blood supply to my foot.

Glenda stayed with John and me in the ER but after Scott saw that I was being taken care of, he went back to the group at the condo. Probably his feet were hurting! At the condo that evening he showed me the blisters on his feet. He had burnt them on the hot slate incline as he was holding the towel giving me shade before the ambulance arrived.

After I woke up from the sedative they gave me before setting the bone, Glenda asked if I had felt anything. I told her, "No, but were a bunch of people in here earlier?" I knew the EMTs had made a couple more runs and stopped in to check on me. John told me that when the doctor was preparing to set the bone they were in the room and had asked if they could watch. (Apparently not much happens in Key West during the day.)

Glenda and John were in the room the entire time. Glenda, skeptical of the doctor's treatment of me, made a great patient advocate. Not only did she insist on the X-ray of my left foot (yep, it was broken too), but she told me that to test that I was sedated, the doctor had poked my eyeball with his finger! Then when he was setting the bone, I sat right up and yelled, "No!" Glenda was afraid I had felt pain during the procedure. John could tell she was about to give the doctor a piece of her mind, but she let it go. During all this Glenda also got on the phone and got a rental wheelchair delivered to the resort for me.

Who breaks both feet on vacation? This girl! After the doctor set the bones back in place on my right foot, he put both feet in an L-shaped splint cast that went from my calf over my heel and along the bottom of my foot. He told us I was going to need surgery within ten days and recommended we contact a surgeon back home.

After four hours in the hospital, we were able to leave, and Scott arrived to drive us back to the resort. John was nervous he was going to hurt me trying to get me in the car. Scott, a muscular six-foot-three, easily picked me up and right in the car I went.

Pain showed up that night. John had volunteered to sleep on the floor so he wouldn't hurt me accidentally. Every time I moved, he got up and checked on me. By Wednesday morning, I was pretty uncomfortable. I think the splint cast hurt more than the injury. The pain medicine made me nauseated.

During the day on Wednesday and Thursday I encouraged John to get outside and be with our friends, so part of the time he stayed with me, but throughout the day our sweet friends took shifts staying with me as well. They prayed for me, watched TV and chatted with me, and even made me milkshakes (the only thing I could hold down because of the medicine). Wednesday afternoon John showed me his phone. He had told some of our friends and family what happened, and his phone was blowing up with dozens of prayers and offers of help.

Somehow John found an orthopedic surgeon with an opening for Friday afternoon, so we left early Friday morning. The six-hour drive was better than I expected: the resort gave us a bunch of pillows, so I rode home like a princess lying in the backseat, legs elevated and completely surrounded by fluffy pillows.

When we got home, John went in first. There in our living room was a wheelchair. John wheeled me in and in the refrigerator, we found a bunch of casseroles and salads and bags of chips and other snacks filling the counter. I knew people had been communicating with John about helping but—Wow! This was overwhelming.

When I met the surgeon, I felt completely safe. I knew he was the doctor I was supposed to have. His voice was soothing, and his touch was so gentle I felt like he was going out of his way to keep from hurting me. The surgery was scheduled for the following Friday, July 26, at two o'clock at a surgery center. The doctor was going to put in a plate, screws and a pin in my right ankle, and a screw in my left foot. "It's an outpatient surgery," he said. "It should take about two hours. And in about six weeks you should be walking normally." He made it sound so simple.

It wasn't simple. The day of the surgery, the doctor was running behind, so they started an hour late. Then, a two-hour surgery took six hours! It turned out I have a bone density problem so the bone wouldn't hold the screws. My doctor had to use the screws as rebar and apply a bone putty to hold everything together. On my right leg, I had thirty staples going up from my ankle on one side and fifteen up the other side. My left ankle had a row of stitches about two inches long where the incision had been. And that six-week recovery became twelve weeks.

While the doctor and his nurses were in surgery with me, John was sitting in the office waiting room with no idea what was happening. At five o'clock the office staff left and he was alone! About six o'clock, when he called the main line, someone did answer and told him I was still in surgery. But no one came out until about eight o'clock to tell him any details. When the nurse woke me up, I was surprised at how much she and the rest of the staff seemed to be hurrying. They practically ran as they put away the surgical tools and supplies. I was thinking, "Gee, it definitely must be after five o'clock," so I asked the nurse what time it was. Ten o'clock!

When the surgeon talked with me after I woke up, I was shocked to learn what had happened. The last bone density test I had taken several years before had been normal. Now I truly felt the Lord had delivered me from something worse. I didn't understand exactly how or why I fell, but I did know that if I had felt myself falling, I would have tensed up and tried to catch myself and caused more damage. I believe something miraculous happened, because other than my broken ankles, I had no bruises, scrapes, or soreness anywhere from falling. Perhaps an angel had caught me and laid me down.

As a side note, kudos to the anesthesiologist! Any time I had had anesthesia in the past, I wouldn't make it home before I got sick, despite their promises of "adding" something to keep that from happening. This anesthesiologist told me the same thing. When I told him I had heard that before, he asked if I suffered from motion sickness. "Yes, I do," I answered.

He said, "That's the reason you've gotten sick; they didn't treat you for that." This surgery was the first time I didn't have any reaction at all! I woke up feeling great. (To those with motion sickness, you're welcome!)

My left foot was in a boot, and the only thing I was allowed to do was pivot with that foot to get in and out of the chair. My right foot was in a splint cast and I couldn't put any weight at all on either foot. Even though I couldn't walk, I considered my blessings: I could still use my arms and I could still work. For the first three weeks I worked in my bedroom. I had to lie in bed, ice packs on my legs, with my legs propped up on pillows. Every day for ten days John gave me a shot in my stomach to keep me from getting blood clots. He also set up a makeshift office in our bedroom. He put my computer and printer on a desk beside me and a friend lent me a tray-like desk (it even had a little light!) that I could set on my lap. One of our friends loaned me a grabber tool—the kind advertised to help people with mobility issues (like me!) reach stuff. I used that to retrieve paper from the printer.

I had forgotten that Holy Spirit had told me, "It's for you," when I had talked about the steps in our townhouse. Now it was coming back to me. He had been telling me something was going to happen, and I wouldn't have to worry about steps. If Holy Spirit had told me I was going to break myself, I know I would have been a nervous wreck just waiting for the other shoe to drop, so to speak. . . .

Holy Spirit showed me how everything had come into place for this experience. Since I lived in Florida, I was already working from home, so that wouldn't change. In God's timing, He had brought our new one-story house to us. Because I'd been involved in our church's Freedom study, God helped me develop the attitude of gratitude I needed to carry me through this challenge. I knew the old me would have been devastated, horrified, and asking, "Why me!?" The old me would have looked at only the negative and would have been miserable and made everyone around me miserable. Instead, I felt incredibly thankful for being delivered from something that could have been a lot worse.

I could control the pain during the day. I would leave our room in the afternoons for a change of scenery or go out to dinner just to get out of the house. Every night, though, the pain came no matter what I did. I cried, prayed, praised, and asked God to relieve the pain. This went on for several nights before I heard Holy Spirit say, "There is pain in healing, but it will get better each day." I felt such compassion from Him, like He understood what I was going through, but also somehow I knew it was for my good for Him not to take the pain away. Holy Spirit changed my perspective. Every night, I would have the pain, but every morning, the swelling in my leg—and the pain—would go down a little. I was keenly aware of my healing process, day by day. It was incredible! I don't even mind the scars—they are a reminder of God's grace.

I went back to church in the wheelchair. John had a place for me up front and over to one side so no one would bump into me. I can't tell you how many people came to me, hugged me, and prayed over me during that time! I lost count of the times I had the opportunity to share what God had done for me. God had used me to turn a negative into a testimony!

I was in the wheelchair when the next baptism weekend came around. It was raining so we changed the location and had a makeshift baptismal set up under cover outside one of the exits. When church let out, I saw my surgeon and his family coming out the door! It's a big church and we hadn't realized he attended Bayside. And normally we would not have been set up in that spot. What are the chances? I had confirmation again that God had brought the right doctor for me.

Our next Freedom group at our house also began shortly after the surgery. This group witnessed the progress I made. When we started, I had both legs in casts and couldn't walk. They watched as I gradually went through different stages with the cast, boot, and crutches. By the end of the group, I could stand and walk with a crutch. Some members of the group told me they could relate their spiritual healing through the study with my physical healing and "walking in freedom." God has given me opportunities at Freedom groups to share what the Lord told me: "There's pain in healing, but it will get better each day."

Several months after my accident we were doing a Freedom group and another new friend from the group brought copies of a book he wanted to share, *You Can Hear the Voice of God,* written by Steve Samson. Immediately I felt drawn to the book. Once I opened it up, I could hardly put it down. Steve includes a chapter in which he talks about the meaning of colors seen in dreams or visions. There it was: "*Pink*—Represents the working power of the Holy Spirit. Pink is a mixture of red (salvation power) and white (the Holy Spirit)."[3]

John's Testimony

Would it be bad to say Donna ruined my vacation? Just kidding!

Our week-long vacation started on a Sunday. On Tuesday, in an odd change of our roles, Donna was the one working from our room and didn't get down to the pool area where the rest of us were until almost lunchtime. I saw her arrive at the pool area but wasn't watching her. I was relaxing in the pool and dozing off a bit. The next thing I knew our friend Becky was yelling for me, and I saw Donna on the ground. Her foot was dangling like a broken branch about to fall off a tree.

---

[3] Steve Samson, *You Can Hear the Voice of God,* [Bloomington, MN: Chosen Books, 2015], 82

Looking back, it's easy to recognize all the things God put in place to help Donna immediately. The stranger who was a nurse that had a bag of ice ready. Scott calmly calling 9-1-1 and making sure Donna had shade while his feet were burning from the heat of the concrete. The medical staff that helped Donna within minutes and hours of the accident. Glenda forcing the issue and making sure the ER doctor X-rayed both feet. Kitty and our other friends caring for her. The medical staff that helped Donna within minutes and hours of the accident.

I'd be lying if I said that I was instinctively calm during the entire situation, but Holy Spirit and the friends and medical professionals around me helped me stay calm. I didn't have to make any decisions because others were acting quickly. Had that not happened, it would have been easy for me to stress over the details. It only took me a couple of minutes to get to the room and back, and by then I could hear the ambulance coming. Donna was completely calm, and help was on the way. Nothing for me to worry about.

Finding Donna a surgeon back home started with a call to Donna's health insurance company, who gave me three suggestions. I quickly Googled them and for some reason the younger doctor stood out—and he had an opening. Seeing the care he gave her on the first visit made it clear Holy Spirit had helped me choose the right one. His not having an appointment available until Friday worked out well because Donna needed a couple of days to rest before making that six-hour drive back home. She also had an ocean-view "recovery room" in Key West. Everyone joined in and showed her love.

Most people wouldn't label me as emotional, but at breakfast the day after Donna's accident everything finally hit me. I prayed for the meal, but as I started praying for Donna's healing, I could no longer speak. Tears started down my cheeks as I was thinking about the pain she was in and wishing we could trade places. Our friend Henry put his arm around me and continued the prayer, asking God to ease Donna's pain and heal her in miraculous time.

Donna has always been tough, and she increasingly bases her joy on the Lord and not her circumstances. Some broken bones didn't stop her from attending dinner out with the group the last night before we left Key West.

When we arrived home Friday afternoon and discovered friends had already filled our refrigerator and freezer and left the wheelchair at the house, we both cried tears of gratitude. We had so much food already that we turned down a meal train our church offered. It was humbling to see the love that was poured out on us and the number of people who reached out wanting to help. We are very blessed by the many friends God has placed in our lives.

Donna was the perfect patient. She didn't complain, didn't play the victim role, and thanked everyone that did anything for her. She could also take a joke. I said, "I figured I would be pushing you in a wheelchair someday but didn't expect it this soon." On numerous occasions I had jokingly told friends that I did everything for her but now I got to see what that really meant. She couldn't put any weight on either foot, so even going to the bathroom was a challenge. But we made it through her months-long recovery together and with the help of many friends.

The accident wasn't our only challenge during this time. Exactly two weeks after Donna's fall, as I had predicted, the offer on our townhouse expired because the buyers didn't sell their house. It felt like we were in a season of storms and sun: Just two weeks after that contract expired, one of the real estate agents who'd shown our house to a client, Sheri, contacted us. She wanted to come look at the townhouse again, but this time, to purchase for herself.

Sheri's house had a contract on it already and she was ready to buy. She loved the townhouse and we agreed on a price. God's timing was at work yet again. When we met to sign the contract, we found out she attended our church, though she hadn't gotten involved in anything other than coming to service. We talked for over an hour and shared how the church and the people were impacting our lives. The whole experience with Sheri felt like a real God story.

Sheri asked for a couple of fixes to be done—a few shingles replaced, a few spots in the gutters repaired—so I started working with the HOA to cover these issues. Friday, August 31, before we left town for Labor Day weekend, we stopped at the townhouse to check if those items had been done. They had not. No problem. I figured I'd check again on the repair progress Tuesday morning after we returned.

By then Donna's left foot was healed and was in a normal shoe but her right foot was still in a cast. Though she mostly used the wheelchair, she sometimes could get around on crutches. This increased mobility came just in time for a much-needed weekend away. It literally felt like a break in a storm.

When I checked on our townhouse after returning though, nothing could have prepared me for the disaster I found.

Self-Reflection

Accidents happen. Problems happen. Knowing Jesus doesn't mean our life is easy, but God is with us. We may not be able to control everything around us, but we *can* control how we react. The sooner we take our concerns to God, the better. Through practice and, more importantly, the help of Holy Spirit, we can fix our eyes on Jesus regardless of the circumstances.

We saw an important lesson in how Scott handled the accident. With his police background, he had the training to handle stressful and emergency situations. But now he was retired. On vacation. Yet that didn't stop his instincts. The gifts God gives us are to be used as a blessing to others, whether we're on vacation or officially on duty.

- Have you ever been in a "Why me?" discussion with God? What do you learn when instead you ask Him, "What were—or are—You trying to teach me?" or "How can I use this as a testimony for others?"

- Are you able to recognize the gifts God has given you to use to bless others? How are you using your gifts? Ask Holy Spirit to help you reflect on this as you read Romans 12:6-8:

  > In his grace, God has given us different gifts for doing certain things well. So if God has given you the ability to prophesy, speak out with as much faith as God has given you. If your gift is serving others, serve them well. If you are a teacher, teach well. If your gift is to encourage others, be encouraging. If it is giving, give generously. If God has given you leadership ability, take the responsibility seriously. And if you have a gift for showing kindness to others, do it gladly.

- Think about the people that have been there for you in a time of need. Lift up a prayer of thanksgiving to God for them.

I have told you all this so that you may have peace in me. Here on earth you will have many trials and sorrows. But take heart, because I have overcome the world.

—John 16:33

Chapter 14

THE FLOOD

John's Testimony

Tuesday, September 4, 2018—The Day after Labor Day.

As I stepped onto our townhouse patio from our detached garage, my foot splashed up water as it hit the ground. It had been raining a bit, so that didn't seem odd at the moment. As I got closer to the back door of our townhouse, the water level was a little deeper. I looked at our back door and saw a stream of water pouring from under the door to the drain on the patio. "That's weird," I thought. I looked up at the gutters to see if maybe it was coming from them. It wasn't.

I unlocked the back door and tried to open it, but it was stuck. When I pulled hard, the door swung open and a wave of water rushed out, splashing over my ankles. In disbelief, I looked up to see water shooting out from the ceiling onto the floor like a garden hose being sprayed at full force through a nozzle. My feet were in two inches of water as I stepped onto the dining room floor. In the area the water was shooting out, the drywall had crashed to the floor and several other areas of the first floor had drywall tape hanging loose and water damage showing.

I screamed out loud, "*Why God?!?* You've put us through the wait and now we're two weeks away from closing and you allow *this* to happen. *Why?*"

I ran up the steps, my feet sloshing across the drenched carpet. In the master bathroom, I found the cause of the flood. The connection from the hose to the toilet was spraying water everywhere. I shut off the valve and fell apart.

Choking on my tears and so full of anger toward God I could barely speak, I called Donna to give her the news. It took me a couple of tries to explain it. She stayed calm and after figuring out what I was telling her, asked if I had called our insurance agent. I hadn't, but giving me a task to do was what I needed.

I talked to our agent, Gail, who was also a close friend, and she walked me through the next steps. A water remediation company would be out in a few hours to get the worst of it up.

I knew I had to call Sheri, our buyer, next.

I was certain that despite the God story of how the sale had happened, she was going to back out. When I told Sheri about the flood, she was silent for what seemed like minutes but was likely only a few seconds. Once the news settled in, she calmly told me she had seen dryouts before, and a deal could still potentially go through. She already had a contractor she trusted lined up for work to do after closing. She was going to paint, replace cabinets, and redo floors. Sheri said, "If you use him for the work, I'll know things will be done right and I'd be comfortable moving forward." We decided to wait a couple of days to let the remediation company get the worst up, then meet to look at what work was needed.

Not having any idea how long the insurance process would take, I told Sheri we would work with her contractor and would not let an insurance payment delay us from being able to close. We'd be sure that the contractor was paid. We had to get creative because all of our equity was in the townhouse. We took out a loan on our car, which we'd previously paid off, and borrowed money from my parents to make sure we could pay for invoices as they came.

Every day something happened to put the closing in jeopardy, but every day God almost immediately delivered a miracle. We found out our HOA insurance covered the drywall replacement, but the morning the drywallers we had already set up arrived, the insurance company put a work stoppage on the job until an appraiser could come. But then after only a one-day delay, the insurance company approved the replacement from the photos we sent them.

The buyer's contractor's price for the cabinet replacements was double what the insurance company was going to pay. But we found another cabinet installer who came in under the insurance price, could get the cabinets and install them in a matter of days, and Sheri agreed to let that contractor do the cabinet work.

During the final walk-through, our hearts sank when we saw a new water spot on the concrete floor in a closet. At first, we thought it was water receding from our neighbor's unit (which was also affected and not completely dry). After calling the cleaning crew, though, we found out they'd used a lot of water on the tile to get the drywall mud off—some had gotten onto the closet's floor and just hadn't dried yet. Life, even with miracles, doesn't always end on a high note. The non-stop highs and lows made those a tiring few days. Tired and exhausted doesn't do justice to how we were all feeling. When we went to the closing, we all looked at each other and agreed, "We want to be excited, but we're just too worn out!"

Remarkably, despite all this and even though the new back door wasn't in yet, Sheri agreed to close the sale. Actually, most of what she had planned to remodel in the townhouse had been covered by our insurance claim, so she was pretty happy. All of this happened within two weeks—we closed on the original date. And, ultimately, the repair costs total came within just twenty dollars of the final payment by the insurance company. Only God!

Donna's Testimony

At one point soon after we discovered the flood, and we were in the midst of lots of bad news, John yelled at me, "I wish you didn't get hurt! I can't do all this by myself!" There was nothing I could do; I didn't have any control over what was happening. I felt attacked but took it to God in prayer. John's roller coaster was up and running! Now on top of everything else he was dealing with, including me just starting to use crutches, he had to figure out a way to pull everything together in time to close.

Let me give you a snapshot of John's life when the offer came in from Sheri. We were making two house payments. My doctor told us I would heal completely, but it would take longer than he first predicted because the bone putty had to solidify to the bone. My left foot, which normally would have healed in three weeks, would now take six weeks. The doctor didn't have a timeline for my right ankle. John was working sixty hours each week, sometimes more, plus handling our normal church responsibilities. From making our meals, to grocery shopping, to getting the mail, he was doing just about everything. Plus, he was taking me to doctor appointments, dealing with the medical bills and the insurance companies. He was feeling the stress for sure.

It had been such a relief when we had signed the offer with Sheri. She told us that she had been praying our townhouse wouldn't sell until she was able to buy it. We joked, "So it's your fault it's taken this long." Again, God was bringing everything together, not just for us, but for her as well.

When John called me after finding the flood when he went to check on the townhouse, I could hardly understand what he was saying. I've learned not to say much when John gets that way. Instead, I pray for Holy Spirit to give him peace. When the timing is right, we can talk things through.

In this case, I wanted to see what had happened to the townhouse for myself. By then I was just starting to walk on my left foot, but unable to put any weight on my right foot. I was on my way down the street on crutches when John came back to get me. Once I got in the front door, I could see parts of the ceiling were gone. The water had poured down the stairs and down the living room wall directly underneath the bathroom. It followed the drywall tape downstairs, starting at the staircase and flowing down every strip from one end of the room to the other, even pouring into the kitchen cabinets.

Every single day, for almost two weeks, we were hit with another piece of bad news, and Holy Spirit and I would pull John off the roof. And every single day, it would all work out. For example, when John called the HOA insurance claim adjuster to approve payment for the drywall replacement, he found out the adjuster, who lived on the coast in North Carolina, was actually evacuating his house right then because a big storm was coming. But it turned out the adjuster's son had played basketball at the University of Louisville, so he and John had an instant connection. In minutes the insurance adjuster knew our whole story and he and John had developed a friendship. Amazingly, the adjuster took care of all the approvals needed before he evacuated!

I was able to stay calm because Holy Spirit had filled me with His peace. I had experienced His grace and faithfulness before, and I was confident everything would work out according to His plan.

John felt we needed to borrow money from his parents and get a loan so he could keep his commitment to Sheri. As it turned out, we didn't need to use his parents' money or the loan. The insurance company came through quickly, and we paid them both off within three weeks.

I love how God turned everything to good! We were still able to close on time and Sheri was able to get exactly what she wanted.

As I reflect back, Holy Spirit showed me how everything came into place. As we mentioned in the introduction, when John said, "I don't have a testimony," I knew there was a story coming that involved me. From the time we prayed for a new house, from hearing that a house without steps was for me, to my accident, to this closing, God had a plan to use this testimony to show His continued faithfulness throughout every aspect of our lives.

I was blessed to be able to recognize God at work throughout these challenges, and to have a peace that only comes from a relationship with Holy Spirit. My past pain has now been replaced with confidence. I know God sees me and is involved in every detail. He doesn't always change my circumstances the way I would want, but His plan will turn everything to good, whether that is on this side of heaven or the other.

My relationship with Holy Spirit, just like any relationship, is always growing. But John and I have both had specific encounters with Holy Spirit that we will never forget. . . .

Self-Reflection

We've all experienced challenging times, when we may feel a flood of emotions from panic and despair to great joy and gratitude. It helps if we keep reminding ourselves that regardless of the specific situation, God is with us during these times, and He has plans for us to use those experiences for His glory.

- Have you ever yelled at God or been angry at Him because of your circumstances? God wants to hear all of our concerns, during both the good and the bad times.

- Have you had peace during a storm like Donna talked about? If not, how can you grow your relationship with Holy Spirit to get to that point?

- Have you been a calming presence during someone else's storm? Think of someone you should reach out to today and be his or her listening ear.

After they prayed, the place where they were meeting was shaken. And they were all filled with the Holy Spirit and spoke the word of God boldly.

—Acts 4:31 (NIV)

Chapter 15

FILLED WITH THE SPIRIT

John's Testimony

The gathering was a call to action. In May 2019, the leaders of the Freedom Ministry scheduled a night of worship and ministry specifically for the volunteers who led small groups or served at the weekends. They challenged everyone to pray for Holy Spirit to prepare our hearts and to get ready for a night of activation and receiving all God had planned for each of us that night. I took that to heart.

I felt this event needed a high level of commitment. That day, I fasted, and only drank water. During the times I normally would have eaten, I spent time reading God's Word and praying, "God, I want to draw closer to you. Open my eyes and my heart. Remove any walls I have put up. Remove any boxes I have put you in. Help me to come tonight ready to receive all that you want to give me." Heading into the event, I had the anticipation of a child waking up on Christmas morning.

The night started with worship music. I couldn't tell you what songs we sang, but I remember being in a level of worship I had never experienced. I felt a connection to God that was new. Praising. Thankful. Excited. God's hand was touching me, and I was physically shaking.

Then came the same prayer time that happens at the weekends. I walked up to Robby, who was one of the leaders. I knew he had been praying for me to walk into everything God had in store for me. I couldn't even speak. As soon as Robby put his hand on my shoulder, I fell to my knees. Holy Spirit fell on me, and I was weeping. I'm not a crier. I certainly don't weep. But I was so overwhelmed by God's presence that I had to release it.

Somehow, I ended up lying flat on the floor. Suddenly I felt the peace of the Lord. As I stood up, I looked around the room and saw others experiencing the presence of Holy Spirit as well. I saw the people there in a completely new way. I felt a love for them as fellow brothers and sisters rather than my normal judgment or comparison. I was changed. And all this happened in the same room that I talked about in the introduction of this book, where I declared, "I don't have a testimony."

I recognize what I have just described is going to rub some people the wrong way. I didn't even put this experience in our first draft of the book. However, keeping it out would mean removing one of the most impactful experiences of my life because I was worried what others would think. I pray my testimony will draw others to Jesus and not away from Him . . . that my experience with Holy Spirit will influence others to talk to Him more . . . to read the Bible more, seeking wisdom about what being filled with the Spirit means.

Acts 13:52 says, "And the disciples were filled with joy and with the Holy Spirit (NIV)." This suggests a continual filling, not a one-and-done. Even the Old Testament speaks to this. Exodus 31:3 says, "I have filled him with the Spirit of God, with wisdom, with understanding, with knowledge and with all kinds of skills (NIV)."

I don't have the answers for how all of this works. I just know I haven't been the same since that day. My eyes can recognize God working in the present, I can lift up praise to Jesus with a full heart, and I can thank Holy Spirit for revealing Himself in new and exciting ways. And I would soon witness God working across the world. . . .

Donna's Testimony

Since the beginning of Freedom when I first realized the voice I had been hearing my entire life was Holy Spirit, I had been praying for both John and me to hear the same messages from Holy Spirit. If I believed Holy Spirit was guiding me, John wouldn't question me, but I wanted him to experience the confirmation from Holy Spirit himself.

That night, at the meeting for Freedom Ministry volunteers, I could feel the presence of Holy Spirit as soon as I walked in the room. It was an overwhelming presence I could physically feel in my body. I was overcome with tears, which is a common response for me. I was hungry for more—to receive everything Holy Spirit had for me. I felt so much love and peace!

During worship, I could see a difference in the way John was engaged. I didn't realize that he had fasted, prayed and prepared for this meeting . . . I just knew something was different. After that night John changed in many subtle—and wonderful—ways. John began letting go of control and letting Holy Spirit take the lead. His attitude toward worship changed, too; he raised his hands during worship and stopped being concerned what others might think. He also began to show more compassion toward others and toward me.

Ephesians 1:13-14 says,

And now you Gentiles have also heard the truth, the Good News that God saves you. And when you believed in Christ, he identified you as his own by giving you the Holy Spirit, whom he promised long ago. The Spirit is God's guarantee that he will give us the inheritance he promised and that he has purchased us to be his own people. He did this so we would praise and glorify him.

We have now led many Freedom groups. Every time we have not only seen transformation in others, but Holy Spirit is still transforming me, peeling layers from me. I see how God had orchestrated our journey to Florida, to this church, and to this study to heal me. He knew I would not have healed in Kentucky. When we arrived at Bayside, the Freedom material did not even exist, but God was working behind the scenes to bring it.

I am so grateful that Jesus gave me Holy Spirit to help me. He's my best friend; I can trust Him. I can tell Him anything and He won't leave me. He has seen me at my worst and still loves me. Because of Him, my life is completely different—and He continues to work in and through me. He took my anger, bitterness, fear, and anxiety and gave me His peace, love, and joy. And He is with me no matter where I go. . . .

Self-Reflection

Were you uncomfortable with this chapter? If so, ask God to help you step outside your box, but with His discernment. Some people, like Donna, are able to do that immediately, while others, like John, take months or years. It's okay to question; in fact, we are called to measure everything we hear against God's Word, but there is no doubt God has more for each of us than we have already seen.

The Freedom program we've talked about is tremendous, but you don't need a special program or a weekend experience to be filled with Holy Spirit. Just ask. Holy Spirit is the perfect gentleman and won't force Himself on anyone. If you have declared Jesus as your Lord and Savior, and you desire a deeper relationship with Holy Spirit whom Jesus left as a gift for all of us, open your hands to receive and ask Holy Spirit to speak to you. Ask to be filled. Ask for a word or vision or feeling to know He is real and wants to be a bigger part of your life. Not every feeling or experience is from God, so align what you experience with the Bible.

- Have you ever asked to be filled with Holy Spirit? If not, will you commit prayer time to do that now? If you have, do you continue to ask to be filled? Will you commit to asking every day for the next week?

- Have you experienced the gifts of Holy Spirit? First Corinthians 12 describes them as wisdom, knowledge, prophecy, faith, healing, working of miracles, discerning of spirits, speaking in tongues, and interpretation of tongues. Which gift will you pray for today?

- Do you walk out your life in the fruit of Holy Spirit? Galatians 5 lists them as love, joy, peace, patience, kindness, goodness, faithfulness, gentleness, and self-control. Which fruit will you pray for more of today?

Lord, you are my God; I will exalt you and praise your name, for in perfect faithfulness you have done wonderful things, things planned long ago.

—Isaiah 25:1 (NLT)

Chapter 16

GOD STORIES AROUND THE WORLD

John's Testimony

Donna and I were having dinner at a restaurant in JFK airport while we waited for our flight to London. Our son Codey and his girlfriend, Jessica, who were planning to join us in London, were still stuck in Louisville—their connecting flight to Charlotte had been delayed. They had a long layover, so they weren't worried. Then their flight was delayed two more times. They started worrying.

I struggled to remain calm. I texted Codey, "God has it under control." But to Donna, I said, "There are no other flights to London tonight. They'll be at least a day behind us if they miss their flight." I checked flight statuses every few minutes, as if knowledge could control the situation.

They took off for Charlotte not knowing if they would make the flight to London. We asked some friends to pray with us that they would make their next flight. Codey and Jessica had to run to the gate, but sure enough, they made it to London about the same time we did.

The idea of a trip to Europe started with Codey. After he spent a summer semester of college in Germany, he really wanted to go back, particularly during Oktoberfest. Donna and I had never been to Europe and loved the idea. We saved for two years and gathered a lot of hotel and flight points (one of the perks of traveling a lot for work and moving timeshare points around). We had enough points to pay for the hotel rooms for all of us, and for the flights for Donna and me. Codey and Jessica had to get to Europe themselves.

Rather than do a tour, we decided to plan every detail ourselves—well, actually, Codey, Jessica and Donna let me handle it. I researched online and talked to some friends who had been to Europe. Our trip turned into a fifteen-day adventure to London; Paris; Rome; Zurich, Switzerland and Munich, Germany.

When I say I planned every detail, I mean I had a spreadsheet with the itinerary that even included what time my alarm would be set for each day. The schedule was packed full so we could see as much as possible. However, most nights did not include a dinner reservation, or anything planned afterward, so we had room to adjust. Every step of the journey, from the planning to getting back home, God was with us. You'll see just how much in Donna's testimony.

Donna's Testimony

I had had the opportunity to go to Germany many years ago when my brother was stationed there while in the Army. He loved it. He told us so many wonderful stories about it. I definitely wanted to go, but unfortunately, that meant I would have had to figure out how to get there and fly *by myself*. Since I was scared of, oh, everything, I didn't go, and instead carried that regret with me. Now I felt like Holy Spirit was telling me this was the time, and I could share it with my son.

Codey and his girlfriend were so anxious about the trip that they got to the terminal in Louisville about four hours before their flight. I can't imagine what they were feeling as the flight continued to be delayed further and further. John was being John, checking the flight times every few minutes, and telling me each scenario that could happen. I wouldn't allow myself to receive what John was saying. In my mind, if flights *to* Charlotte were delayed, then flights *from* Charlotte would be as well. When they finally left Louisville, they thought they would be landing about the time their connecting flight was leaving. It wasn't until they landed in Charlotte that they found out their connecting flight was delayed as well. What a blessing!

Before we left for Europe, several of our friends prayed over us. Wendy, from the Feed My Sheep ministry, prophetically told us there would be a woman we would encounter. She saw her with an orange, shiny fabric of some kind. At first, I wondered, "How are we going to know who this is? What if we miss the opportunity?" I left thinking we were supposed to show the love of God to others. It wasn't long before I realized God wanted to show His love to us.

God was in the details. Every time something would happen, He was there! For example, our whole trip was on John's phone, including routes to take, confirmations for events, everything! When we were in Paris, the charge on his phone got low and he pulled out his portable charger. For some reason, it hadn't charged! He was trying to figure out what to do, and right then a man came down the street selling chargers. The whole trip was like that. Any problem that popped up was taken care of just as quickly. I could see God's favor over us, protecting us the whole time.

My most memorable "mom moment" happened at the Basilica of The Sacred Heart (known as the Church on the Hill) overlooking the city of Paris. I could feel the presence of Holy Spirit when I walked into the church. I sat down in a pew and started to pray. Codey came in and sat down beside me; we just held hands and took it all in. My heart was full!

While the others were looking forward to Oktoberfest, I was dreading it. My brother had talked about the crazy things that happened there. I didn't want to spend several days in a beer tent watching people do things I wouldn't be able to un-see.

We arrived on opening day, which I felt sure would be even crazier. We watched the parade, which consisted of people waving from horse-drawn, decorated wagons carrying the kegs of beer going to Oktoberfest. Crowds of people, dressed in their lederhosen and other traditional German attire, followed the parade, and headed into the tents.

We had been sitting in a beer tent an hour or so when we noticed a cheery lady from the table behind us. She got up and danced by herself, then with a waitress, and, finally, her husband. John took a picture of the happy couple and offered to send her the picture. When we began chatting, she complained her knee was hurting. John closed his eyes to pray privately, and she asked if he wanted to pray over her. He said, "Sure, we can do that."

She mentioned that when she was young and had a health problem, someone prayed over her, and she was healed. She said, "I'm not much on religion, but you can pray in whoever's name you want." We prayed with her and turned back to our table.

A few minutes later, she tapped me on the shoulder and said, "I know it's working, I can feel it."

I told her, "God is good!"

We continued talking. She had been raised Christian, but clearly was struggling with her faith. She mentioned (referring to Abraham and Isaac), that "her God" wouldn't tell someone to kill their son and then at the last minute say, "I'm just kidding." I just let her talk and get everything off her chest and silently prayed as she spoke.

An hour or so later, she tapped me on the shoulder again. She said, "I need you to pray again, I think I need more."

Immediately, I heard Holy Spirit say, "She's opening the door to let Me in." This time, I prayed not only for healing, but for Holy Spirit to fill her. She hugged me and tears were coming down her face. I knew He touched her! Wow! When John sent Wendy, our friend from Feed my Sheep, the lady's picture, Wendy replied, "That's what I saw, the orange scarf wrapped around her waist!" Praise God!

I don't know how many times John had gone back and forth to the restroom throughout the day, or why he had our passports in his back pocket, but at one point someone tapped John on the shoulder and pointed down. Our passports were on the ground! They could have fallen out anywhere, and we would have not even known where to begin to look. We never did see any craziness at Oktoberfest, and, passports in hand, we made it home with no problems. Thank God!

John's Testimony

About five months after our Europe trip, we found out early on a Saturday morning that our close friend Scott, who had been so helpful during Donna's accident, had lost his battle with cancer. We had visited Scott and Glenda in Louisville a few times and had seen Scott's struggle. While we were in town for

162

the funeral, another friend posted on Facebook that someone had an item they needed picked up in Knoxville and brought to Florida, and wondered if anyone would be in the area and interested in making a little money for the trouble. Donna and I weren't sure exactly when we would be driving back, and rerouting through Knoxville would add at least another hour and a half to an already long trip, but the post caught my attention.

The item was a 1957 American Standard bass guitar that was going to be used during an acoustic worship set at our church. The sellers were raising money to purchase their first home and we love seeing people achieve that goal. I still wasn't thrilled with the inconvenience of the side trip, but Holy Spirit worked on me. I was hearing about some expenses Glenda was concerned about and a few things from her husband's retirement that were not working out like expected. I realized that for a few hours of our time, we could donate to her whatever the person was paying. So, I told the buyer we would do it.

If the story ended there it would still be a nice testimony, but then another person heard the money was going to a widow and offered to match the delivery fee with a donation. Following that, another person heard about the situation and donated double of those two amounts together. The original delivery fee turned into a donation to Glenda that was SIX times larger, which happened to be the exact amount of a car repair bill she had just told Donna about.

Donna's Testimony

Our friend Scott had been battling cancer for well over a year. At 2:00 a.m. on a Saturday morning in February 2020, Glenda called to say it wouldn't be long. John was already scheduled to be out of town the whole week, so he knew he wouldn't be able to go with me to be with Glenda. He was looking up flights for me to go and asking me to make a decision on flight times. We had just been awakened by Glenda's call, and he wanted to know right then. I asked him to wait. I heard Holy Spirit say, "Drive," but John was convinced I should fly. It's at least a fourteen-hour drive and I would be going by myself. I was okay with that; I've driven long distances several times by myself. At that time, though, I was focused on praying for them.

At 4:00 a.m., Glenda's sister called to tell us Scott was in heaven. John asked me again if I wanted to fly. I told him I would drive. Later that day, John said his boss told him he was still needed that week, but he could change his return flight to fly into Kentucky Wednesday night in time for the funeral on Thursday. John agreed if I drove, we wouldn't have to worry about return flight times; we could just return when we chose to. (Confirmation!) I'm so thankful God worked everything out so we could be with Glenda during this time.

I packed some snacks and drove to Kentucky. For the first time since we moved, I didn't run into any construction or traffic jams (even through Atlanta), and I made it in thirteen hours. When I got to Louisville, I found out Glenda's car was in the shop, so we used mine. Obviously, this was another reason I was led to drive, but there was still more.

John arrived Wednesday night and asked if I had seen the post from a friend asking a favor from anyone that happened to be in the Knoxville area. I thought, ". . . And here we are, close to Knoxville. What a coincidence!" I wanted to help our friend but didn't say anything to John. At first, John didn't seem interested in picking up the guitar, but Holy Spirit worked on him until he was convinced we needed to do it. (This is a good reminder that Holy Spirit is much more effective in changing our spouses than we are.) How all the details of this trip played out was so God! He worked everything out for good. We were able to bless Glenda and our guitar-owner friend. We left early Saturday morning, and again, had no problems on the road. We got home that same night.

Two days later we were headed to Israel.

John's Testimony

Monday morning we left with a group from church on a spiritual retreat to Israel. In preparation for the trip, we had daily Scripture readings and were lifted up in prayer by friends. We also read Kathie Lee Gifford's book, *The Rock, the Road, and the Rabbi,* which helped us learn more history about the places we would be seeing. It also explains the significance and meaning of Jewish traditions mentioned in Scripture. It was an inspiration for how we wrote this book, with both of us writing our testimony each chapter. Kathie co-wrote with Rabbi Jason Sobel.

Our God stories from this trip start at the airport in Tampa, Florida. I was flying so much that I had TSA pre-check and had gotten it for Donna as well. We usually fly Delta, which would have given me pre-check automatically, but the church planned the trip, and we were flying United. I didn't even think to look at the ticket. When Donna and I entered the TSA line, I was informed that I didn't have pre-check. I went to the regular line where a large party of people slowed down our processing. I also forgot to take my CPAP out of my bag (because with pre-check I usually don't have to), and I was delayed again. When I finally got through, Donna walked up. She was wearing a shirt that said "faith" on it. The TSA agent told Donna that more people needed to publicly profess their faith in God. When she found out we were headed to Israel, she pulled us aside and prayed over us. Donna returned the favor and prayed for her and her family as well. This is a great reminder that often when we are sidetracked, God has something in store for us.

The church brought along a production crew because they were going to film the pastor's message for Easter, along with capturing our trip. I wasn't sure about the idea of the Easter message being a video. Our church had used video messages in the past, but Easter is a different story. God had a plan there too. In 2020, because of COVID-19, our church canceled live services for a time. Live services for Easter weren't happening so our Easter service ended up entirely digital anyway. Being there in Israel with our pastor as he recorded the service made it an Easter service I will never forget.

In Israel, I didn't have to plan a thing. The church did a perfect job. We saw a ton of places, but our days weren't packed full. We were able to spend time alone with God at each stop. This trip was so moving and inspiring, we could write an entire book about it. For me, a few of the highlights were sailing on the Sea of Galilee (where Jesus walked on water and calmed the storm), the Southern Steps (where Jesus and the disciples would have walked into the City of David on what is now Palm Sunday), the Garden of Gethsemane (where Jesus was betrayed), and the Garden Tomb (one of the possible locations Jesus was buried).

We had the perfect tour guide who explained the history of each site and its place in the Bible, and shared his personal testimony as well. At many of the stops, several pastors in our group also shared what God placed on their heart. We also heard a portion of a talk Pastor John Maxwell, the world-renowned speaker and author, gave at a local church. On our bus each morning, a powerhouse leader and public speaker handled the devotion for our group.

Scholars debate the exact location Jesus was buried, but our tour guide had the perfect comment on the issue: "The important thing is that the tomb is empty." Praise God that Jesus is risen! So, while I can't tell you with any certainty where Jesus was buried, I can tell you the Garden Tomb is a special place to me. We had communion near the site and the prayer time was powerful. As I was walking out of the tomb, one of our group's pastors pulled me aside and asked if I would handle the morning devotion the day before we left for home. My mind was on what Jesus had done for us, so how could I say no?

After only a few moments, though, I began to question. The bus was full of people far more qualified and better speakers than I am. Why in the world did the pastor ask me? I should have known by then that it had nothing to do with what I was capable of. It had to do with what God planned to do through (and to) me.

I'm a great sleeper. When my head hits the pillow, I'm out in seconds. Many times I have asked Donna a question and then fallen asleep before she has a chance to answer. That night, while thinking about what I should do for the devotion, I lay in bed for two hours listening to Holy Spirit download what he wanted me to say. When I woke up in the morning, I typed it all out. I connected the visit we would have that day to Nazareth, Jesus' hometown, and related that to us returning home. Holy Spirit would be giving us matchless opportunities to bring others closer to Him. People were going to ask how our trip to Israel went. Would we say the hotels were great and the sites were beautiful, or would we talk about how God spoke directly to us while we were there?

The devotion went well. I did a decent job of staying out of the way, letting Holy Spirit speak through me. Taking this full circle, what I wrote in the introduction to this book, about declining to speak to Celebrate Recovery, feeling unqualified to speak, and saying "I don't have a testimony," I included in that devotion.

Donna's Testimony

Our visit to Israel was the most amazing trip I've ever experienced. Reading events in the Bible and then seeing where they happened completely changed my perspective. I tried to imagine what Jesus experienced while walking in the

Garden of Gethsemane, where He went to pray and was betrayed, and the Mount of Olives, where He could see Jerusalem and wept for her. A highlight for me was our boat ride on the Sea of Galilee. The surroundings were so beautiful and peaceful, and just sitting in the boat, taking it all in, was a deeply spiritual experience. The Garden Tomb was another impactful site. One of our pastors, giving a message there, reminded us that the blood of Jesus literally poured into the ground in Jerusalem, and was still crying out for all of us. Then we took communion. It was so powerful!

The City of Old Jerusalem is still surrounded by walls, and divided into four quarters: Jewish, Muslim, Armenian, and Christian. On Shabbat, which is the Jewish Sabbath, everything shuts down. Even in our hotel, the employees made preparations ahead of time, so they could follow the laws set for Shabbat. Our pastor arranged for a local family to come to our hotel to show us how they celebrate. We could also hear singing throughout the hotel as other families were celebrating as well.

The Western Wall (or wailing wall) is the closest, geographically, that Jews can get to the original site of the temple without being under Islamic jurisdiction. It was so moving to see all the prayers tucked into cracks, and lines of men and women praying. With my modern, American perspective, I was surprised to see that there are separate sections for men and women. The women's section is all outside. The men's section has an indoor area and is at least five times larger.

The relationships we formed with our pastors and friends, old and new, were incredible. I loved the excitement and joy the pastors displayed as they hung out with us and described the role the places we were visiting played in the Bible. We even had the opportunity to just sit around a fire and share stories.

On a lighter note, there was a JFC! Yes, Jerusalem Fried Chicken. Some teenagers were inside when we stopped in front of it to take a picture. Their curiosity got the best of them, and they asked why we were interested. We told them we were from Kentucky and wanted to see if theirs tasted like KFC's. They peeked back in after we sat down to eat and asked if it did. We said, "No, not even close." They laughed and said, "We didn't think so!"

You may recall that when I was baptized at age nine, I wasn't clear what being baptized meant. On this trip we had the opportunity to be baptized at the Jordan River! For some reason, I was overcome with anxiety about it, like I was doing something wrong. Then I felt peace when I heard Holy Spirit say, "This time, when you are baptized, you really know who I am!"

Self-Reflection

In the busyness of everyday life, it's easy to look past everything God is doing. However, it's important to pause and marvel at the things He puts in place for us.

You don't have to go Europe, Kentucky, or Israel; God can connect to each of us wherever we are. It was extraordinary to get away from the distractions and demands of daily life and walk on the same roads Jesus did. But a walk along the beach or in the woods could be just as impactful.

- Where do you find it easiest to spend quiet time with God? Perhaps the beach, the woods, or a prayer closet. If it's not on your schedule already, plan some time now for your next conversation.

- Do you take time to think about the details God puts in place each day? Do you keep a journal? We encourage you to write your testimonies down. It will make it easier for you to recall them and share them with someone else when the time is right.

- Our church's pastors are required to take time off for spiritual growth. Is there somewhere you have considered going for a spiritual retreat you haven't committed to yet? Will you commit to making those plans?

Open my lips, Lord, and my mouth will declare your praise.

—Psalm 51:15 (NIV)

Chapter 17

TELL YOUR STORY

John's Testimony

I f this book helps one person, it was worth our time to write. Only God knows where this will lead. Fortunately for us, we have been blessed to know it's already made a difference. While we were writing this, a coworker of mine was devastated to learn her husband had cancer. One morning, right as I was reviewing Donna's testimony about the spirit of fear, my coworker messaged me about her struggles. I sent her Donna's words, and she wrote back, "That's me! I can totally relate to that exact fear! I am going to read this several times and really let this into my brain, but more importantly my heart. I simply cannot wait for your book to be published. Thank you, and of course your wife, for this inspirational piece!" It never ceases to amaze me how God is always listening, watching, and protecting us. He directs traffic and puts people and circumstances in our lives at just the moment they are needed.

I never stop being amazed at how often I have shared part of my testimony with someone and there is no doubt it was a divine appointment. If you read the acknowledgments, you will see we thanked our friend Nate Kneser for his help with our book, but let me tell you how we met. It was the Friday night session of a Freedom Weekend in 2019. I was outside with a couple of other volunteers getting the baptism area prepared. The session was almost over, and people would soon be coming out.

Nate and his fiancée were the first to arrive. I had never met them before, but I asked if they knew anyone getting baptized. Nate said, "No. I haven't seen a baptism at this church and thought I would watch." Others started walking up as well. I think eight people were baptized that night and at least forty gathered to help celebrate.

When Freedom Weekend continued the next morning, I saw Nate getting coffee. Holy Spirit nudged me to go talk to him. I thought, "Why? I don't even know him. What am I supposed to say?" Finally, I just did it. I walked up and asked what he thought of the baptism the night before.

Nate said something along the lines of, "Well, it was different than I'm used to." He wasn't attacking anything, but I could tell he wasn't comfortable with the way our church practiced baptism. I told him that I understood, and that I had wrestled with the theology of baptism for years before I ultimately decided to be baptized by immersion. I told him my dad was a Lutheran pastor and it was different from the way I was taught too.

Nate said, "Wow. My dad is a Lutheran pastor." Our fathers were even in the same synod and went to the same college at one point. We talked a little longer, exchanged numbers so we could connect for coffee sometime, and went into the Saturday session of Freedom.

After the session, I talked to Nate a little more. He brought up a few things that caught his attention, and we had a short discussion with one of the pastors about how our church handled essential and non-essential beliefs. Nate was extremely interested in "why" our church does things the way they do.

This was the last public gathering at our church before services were moved online because of COVID-19. Nate and I texted a few times, but there was nowhere to meet for coffee since everything had been closed.

I next contacted Nate after Donna and I had a zoom meeting with a couple of our pastors who had written books. They suggested we have someone that we either didn't know or didn't know well read our book. At first, I wondered how in the world we were going to find that person, but after a few days, Holy Spirit put Nate on my heart.

I sent him a text saying, "Let me ask you an odd question. Are you a reader? Donna and I have started writing a book. Not a lot of people know, and we have no idea what we are doing. We were advised to have a few different people read as we go that may have different perspectives. I think you may be perfect.

Don't feel obligated but I'll send an introduction to the book to see if you are interested."

Nate told me that he had recently started reading more and had been passionate about "everyone has a story" for the last several years as well. He immediately started asking good questions and was invaluable in the book writing process. It's been fun to see some of the similarities of our testimonies. It's also amazing how God planned all this long ago.

Part of my testimony is embarrassing. Sometimes it can be awkward to bring up some of these details with people I don't know well. However, if I let Holy Spirit lead, my story can be exactly what a person needs to hear. It's humbling to think my story could bring hope, healing, and joy to someone else, but then I remember—my story is God's story.

Donna's Testimony

God is all about connecting with us. He wants to be involved in every aspect of our life. Nothing is too big or too small to share with God. I remember a trip back to Louisville about nine months before Scott's passing. John wasn't with me. I didn't want to walk alone into the church and search for someone to sit with. I was praying as I was getting off the expressway and took the wrong exit! I was headed the back way to church and didn't know which street to take. While I was looking for a familiar street name, I heard my friend Dee Dee's car (a Mustang GT convertible) before I saw her turning into my lane ahead of me. I followed her the rest of the way to church and parked close to her. Dee Dee had stuff in her trunk to unload and take in, so I was able to help her and sit with her family. How cool is that!? As John said above, God literally directs traffic and puts people in our lives at just the right moment.

God is all about partnering with us to connect others as well. The best example happened that same week with our friend Scott. He was big in stature and heart. Scott never met a stranger and it seemed like he knew just about everyone in Louisville.

When he found out he had cancer, Scott's faith was shaken. He said he couldn't believe God would give him cancer. I didn't think he would accept it from me if I tried to explain to him that the cancer was not from God, so I prayed for God to bring someone to him that he would respect and listen to.

While at church that Sunday, Dee Dee, Steve (John's mentor) and I agreed to meet for dinner on Tuesday. On Tuesday morning, as I had been doing daily, I prayed for Scott. This time I asked God to bring someone to him, and I heard Holy Spirit say clearly, "Steve is your person." I burst into tears. Steve, a wise and godly friend, was perfect. But Scott and Steve didn't know each other well. I didn't know how God was going to bring the two guys together, but I knew I needed to let Steve know what Holy Spirit said.

I thought Scott had to work the night of the dinner, so I only invited Glenda, Scott's wife, to dinner with Steve and Dee Dee. Glenda didn't commit to coming. When I was waiting in the parking lot of the restaurant for Steve and Dee Dee, my phone rang. Glenda and Scott were on their way to meet us for dinner! That dinner was the start of the connection Holy Spirit had told me about.

During the last few months of Scott's life, Steve kept in contact with him and helped Scott develop a new relationship with Jesus. There is no question that Scott is in heaven! When John and I went to Louisville for Scott's funeral, one of Scott's friends said, "You know, the last few months Steve was the only person Scott would really talk to." Sometimes our purpose is to connect the right person at the right time.

When we started writing this book, I didn't realize all the times God had shown up in my life. I hadn't thought about a lot of it, buried some of it, and really hadn't spoken of it. Through the process of writing the book, I have experienced healing I didn't know I needed. (Don't tell John . . . lol!) Only God knows how you will benefit from telling your testimony.

As John mentioned, our writing this book has impacted people already. Here's another instance: Remember the waitress from the Introduction? She waited on us when we went to the restaurant to work on chapter one. I had given her my number, but didn't hear from her, and then COVID-19 hit. Several months later, John and I were back at that restaurant working on our last chapter and guess who our waitress was? She had lost my number, and when the restaurants closed, had gone to Georgia to stay with her parents. She had moved back just a few days earlier. This time she gave me her number and told me she would love to join my ladies' small group!

Self-Reflection

Let's not forget the greatest testimony of all time: The Testimony, lived out by our Lord and Savior Jesus Christ. It is because of what He did that we have hope and eternal life. He fulfilled the law, He died on the cross, rose on the third day, and now sits at the right hand of God ruling His kingdom. Our stories are a part of His master story, and it is through Jesus' testimony that we are saved through grace.

We can't stress enough how important it is to share your testimony with others.

When we focus on what God has done in our lives, amazing things happen. By sharing our testimony with others, we are praising God for what He has done. God-stories encourage us all, and frequently they can be exactly what a specific person needs to hear at just the right time.

We all have a story, and we believe when you look back, you'll see where God has been there for you too. God is always with us whether we recognize it or not. We also believe someone else needs to hear your story to make sense of some things.

Thank you for reading our testimonies. We hope you have been blessed and encouraged to see how God has worked in our lives. God has a plan for you as well. Our prayer is that your eyes, ears, and heart will be open to receive what He has in store for you, and then you will share your story!

- What's your story?

- Have you written it down? If not, commit to taking thirty minutes today to start writing it. Then do it.

- Who needs to hear your story? Pray for God to reveal the answer.

We would love to hear from you, whether it be to share part of your story that you've never shared before, to let us know how this book helped you, or to respond to some of the points we've made.

You can reach us at testimonyispraise@gmail.com or visit us at:

www.testimonyispraise.com
www.youtube.com/testimonyispraise
www.facebook.com/testimonyispraise

Twitter - @TestimonyPrais
Instagram – TestimonyIsPraise

ACKNOWLEDGMENTS

We have to start by thanking God, because this book is His book. He gave us the vision to write it, the connections to help us, and of course, He was there alongside us when the testimonies we have written about happened.

If it weren't for Janice Buckson prophesying over us, our original small outline would still be in a Word document in a file. We can't thank you enough for listening to God's prompting to speak over us, and encouraging us as we wrote the first draft.

Thank you to Pastors Alex and Kim Anderson. They were great mentors at the beginning of the process and connected us with our writing coach and editor.

To our writing coach and editor, and now our friend, Maureen Guffanti. When you read our first draft, you gave honest feedback that it was "a nice journal." The final product has been dramatically improved by your hard work and prayers.

Thank you to Oleg Atbashian, who skillfully handled the cover and formatting. We didn't even know where to start!

To our good friend, Nate Kneser. We appreciate your attention to every word and our contextual uses of Scripture. Your questions and suggestions were challenging—in a good way.

We give thanks for the many friends and family that read through various versions. Kevin and Jennifer Kaminski, Andy and Christine Fowler, Brad and Lori Willy, Pastor David and Susan Kipp, Steve Gibson, Pastor Sean Callaghan, and Michael and Victoria Eastman. We'll be forever grateful for your help, guidance, endorsements, and prayers.

We found our cover picture online and give thanks to David Choate for allowing us to use it. To us, that picture captures so beautifully the testimonies of life.

Finally, we give thanks for the many people that have prayed for us during this process. Prayer changes things. We are blessed beyond measure to have all of you in our lives.

Appendix A
TIPS FOR WRITING YOUR TESTIMONY

- Spend time in prayer. Ask Holy Spirit to reveal to you what to write. We started with an outline of our lives and identified the key areas we recognized God at work.

- Schedule time to write. If it isn't on the schedule, it won't get done.

- Don't worry about the first draft being perfect. Just get your thoughts down on paper.

- Tie Scripture into your testimony.

- Be specific. Consider writing it like a story, with dialogue and specific details, including location and dates. Try to include how you felt.

- Had we kept daily journals, this process would have been much easier. We encourage you to start that practice.

- After writing drafts, seek advice from friends and family.

- Even if you aren't ready to share your story with the world, still write it out. As Donna mentioned, the process helped her heal in many areas.

- Everyone has been hurt at some point in their lives. It's important to heal your hurts, and talking or writing about your experiences helps. In our writing, we tried to avoid focusing on the mistakes of others—we encourage you to see those that hurt you as God sees them: children beloved of God, who are struggling with pain themselves.

- If co-writing with your spouse, remember patience and grace. . . .

Appendix B
ADDITIONAL RESOURCES

- If you're looking for a church home, see Robert Verlarde's article: "Looking for the 'Right' Church?" at https://www.focusonthefamily.com/faith/looking-for-the-right-church/.

- To dive deeper into who Holy Spirit is and how you can have a relationship with Him, we recommend the books *The God I Never Knew* by Robert Morris and *The Holy Spirit* by John Bevere.

- To learn more about how you can hear from God, read *You Can Hear the Voice of God* by Steve Samson.

- Two of John's favorite leadership books are *Leader Shift* by John Maxwell and *Amplified Leadership* by Dan Reiland.

- Planning a trip to Israel or wanting to connect the Bible more to Israel? Read *The Rock, the Road, and the Rabbi* by Kathie Lee Gifford and Rabbi Jason Sobel.

- If you want to write your own testimony, we recommend reading *I Can Only Imagine* by Bart Millard.

- To dive deeper in your prayer life, read *Dangerous Prayers* by Alex Anderson.

- If you're wondering what your purpose is, read *The Purpose Driven Life* by Rick Warren.

- Three books Donna recommends from her women's small group are *When Wallflowers Dance* by Angela Thomas, *The Armor of God* by Priscilla Shirer, and *Girls With Swords* by Lisa Bevere.

- For a devotional to help your marriage, we suggest *The Love Dare* by Alex Kendrick.

- Finally, and most importantly, make it a daily habit to go to the written Word of God, The Bible. We recommend the New Living Translation (NLT) or New International Version (NIV) translation. Consider using a Bible reading plan at https://www.biblegateway.com/reading-plans/.

Made in United States
Orlando, FL
23 January 2022